The Power of
PRAYING®
THROUGH
Fear

STORMIE
OMARTIAN

HARVEST HOUSE PUBLISHERS
EUGENE, OREGON

Cover by Bryce Williamson

Cover Image © axllll /iStock

Back cover author photo © Michael Gomez Photography

Italics in quoted Scriptures indicates emphasis added by the author.

THE POWER OF PRAYING® THROUGH FEAR
Copyright © 2017 by Stormie Omartian
Published by Harvest House Publishers
Eugene, Oregon 97402
www.harvesthousepublishers.com

ISBN 978-0-7369-6595-8 (pbk.)
ISBN 978-0-7369-6596-5 (eBook)

Library of Congress Cataloging-in-Publication Data
Names: Omartian, Stormie, author.
Title: The power of praying through fear / Stormie Omartian.
Description: Eugene, Oregon : Harvest House Publishers, [2017]
Identifiers: LCCN 2017029355 (print) | LCCN 2017036193 (ebook) | ISBN 9780736965965 (ebook) | ISBN 9780736965958 (pbk.)
Subjects: LCSH: Fear—Religious aspects—Christianity. | Prayer—Christianity.
Classification: LCC BV4908.5 (ebook) | LCC BV4908.5 .O43 2017 (print) | DDC 242/.4—dc23
LC record available at https://lccn.loc.gov/2017029355

Printed in the United States of America

17 18 19 20 21 22 23 24 25 / BP-JC / 10 9 8 7 6 5 4 3 2 1

God has not given us a spirit of fear,
but of power and of love
and of a sound mind.

2 Timothy 1:7

Contents

Say What?

Much is written in the Bible about the words we say and whether we speak the truth or a lie. Some people speak a lie to themselves over and over so many times that they start to believe it, and then it becomes true for them. In other words, they talk themselves into believing what they want to believe. Other people believe a lie without realizing it because they don't know what the real truth is. But real truth survives and ultimately wins out. So people who speak a lie, or believe a lie, can only live on that false premise for so long until the truth surfaces—which it eventually will because real truth never dies.

This book is about finding the Truth—with a capital T—concerning our fears and then learning to speak the truth until our heart and mind accept and believe it wholeheartedly. It's about praying to know the truth that sets you free and then taking the necessary steps to receive all the freedom God has for you.

In order to live the life God has for us, we cannot allow our fears to control us.

In the following chapters are tools to help you not only discover your own hidden fears and face them, but also to build a strong foundation of scriptural truth upon which you can stand in order to get completely free of them. Included are steps you can take immediately, at the first fear-filled thought you have, to help you identify the kind of fear God *allows*, and how that can be a good thing. Also, there needs to be in all of us a clearer understanding of the only kind of fear God *wants* you to have—and how to live accordingly. There are also lists of powerful thoughts and words you can quickly and deliberately *think*, *say*, and *pray* when you are struggling with fear of any kind that will help you overcome it. And there are many things you can *do* whenever fear threatens to take away your peace that will help restore calm to your soul, as well as prevent the debilitating aspects of fear. The most common fears, such as fear of rejection, fear of failure, fear of pain, fear of loss, fear of insignificance, fear of evil, fear of death, and fear of the future can affect our lives more than we may think. When we conquer these major fears, the rest of our fears will lose their power as well. And that is what I pray for you and everyone who reads this book.

Stormie Omartian

1

What Can Fear Do to Us?

If I could sum up the first 30 years of my life in one word, it would be FEAR. That's because I experienced so many terrifying things when I was a child that fear carried over into adulthood. I never had anyone to talk to about what was happening to me, or who could reassure me that things would get better, or who would help me feel safe, so fear became a way of life for me.

We all experience some kind of fear in our lives. Each one of us is afraid of something. We know fear to be the familiar feeling that comes as a result of believing certain persons, situations, or conditions might threaten our well-being, or the well-being of those we love and care about the most. Other words that describe fear are dread, anxiety, apprehension, alarm, agitation, panic, worry, deep concern, or terror. Show me an honest person—one reasonably in touch with reality—who never experiences any of these emotions. I have actually heard people say, "I don't have fear. I just have some anxiety, dread, worry, and occasional panic attacks." I feel like saying, "Hello! Fear is the root of all of that!" But I don't want to scare anyone.

There is much to be afraid of in this world because no place is completely safe. We only need to turn on the news to see reasons we may have to be frightened. And the evil behind them is increasingly horrifying. That's why fear in the heart of many people appears to be at an all-time high. It's an emotional epidemic.

Besides all the *external* reasons to have fear, we suffer just as much from the fears that come from *within* us. And those fears can interfere with our life more than we may even realize. They could be caused by bad memories of fearful things that happened in the past, and we fear they could happen again at any moment. Or we may have had these fears for so long that we don't even know why anymore. We may even think, *This is just the way I am—anxious, overly concerned, and apprehensive.*

Whatever the reason, fear affects us mentally, emotionally, and physically. It weakens us and makes us sick in our mind, body, and soul. It shackles us. It interferes with our relationships and work. It can build within us until we become emotionally paralyzed by it. When we believe there is no way out of a terrifying or threatening situation for an extended period of time, that belief can affect every part of us with fear that leaves us incapacitated.

When we are fearful, we lose our joy, energy, and strength—especially if fear has been with us long term. If we don't do something to either remove the threat or remove *ourselves* from the threatening situation, fear will affect us in countless negative ways and take away more from our life than we may even know.

Panic and anxiety, for example, can freeze your mind so that you cannot think straight. Fear can emotionally incapacitate you until you are unable to act in a calm and rational manner. Fear affects your health so that your blood pressure rises and your heart beats so hard you constantly hear it and feel it pulsing in your ears. It can make you feel as if you are dying. I know this because I experienced paralyzing fear, anxiety, and panic attacks so intrusive I didn't know if I could pull it together to do even the simplest things I needed to do.

When we experience such perpetual fear that it becomes a controlling force in our life, it makes us feel as if life is *out* of control. When fear takes over our life like that, it keeps us from moving into all we can be and do. A person can still experience symptoms of great fear even when what caused that fear in the first place is long gone. Anyone who has had extreme and traumatic long-term fear can become dangerously affected by it if not treated properly.

The Bible describes fear that is sudden and uncontrollable in this way: "*Fear took hold of them* there, and pain, as of a woman in birth pangs" (Psalm 48:6). When fear takes hold of us suddenly, we can be painfully overwhelmed by it, and it can be disabling, just like birth pangs for a woman. At its worst, this kind of fear can become a phobia if not addressed effectively over a long period of time.

I used to be controlled by fear and anxiety the way I just described to the point of emotional and physical paralysis. But I'm not that way anymore. I learned a long time ago that this kind of destructive and incapacitating fear doesn't come from God. It's part of the plan the enemy of our soul has for us, and we must come to know the truth that sets us free. The absolute truth is, God will never give us a spirit of fear. He has given us His *power*, His *love*, and nothing less than a *sound mind*. Those things are more than enough to help us be free from a spirit of fear.

My early childhood, from as far back as I can remember, set me up for a life controlled by a spirit of fear. I experienced one frightening situation after another because my mother was severely mentally ill. She was also very angry, sinister, and mean. She was changeable in an instant, depending on who was around. It seemed that her favorite thing to do to me when I was a small child was slap me hard in the face when I least expected it and lock me in a small, dark closet underneath the stairs in the old two-story ranch house we lived in. She called me filthy names—most of which I will never in my life repeat to anyone. They are sickening, degrading, embarrassing, and offensive to any person who would read or hear them. She did all these things for reasons only she knew, because I never understood what I had done to deserve her wrath.

The lack of love and compassion from her, and her violence and hatred toward me, made me terrified, anxious, and afraid all the time. We were isolated on a small ranch in Wyoming, 20 miles from the nearest town and miles from the closest neighbors. We had no heat except what came from a small fireplace in the tiny living room or the wood-burning stove in the even smaller kitchen. We had no electricity and no plumbing, so there were no lights or running water. Everyone else had all those things, so it wasn't the way people lived at the time. We were poor and couldn't afford anything more.

We did have a well from which my dad drew water to drink. Any water to bathe in had to be heated up on the stove and poured into a tin tub. It was too much work for my father to do very often because he worked hard just to barely eke out a living. He was also gone a lot working in logging mills in order for us to survive.

To make matters worse, rattlesnakes were around in abundance, some of which came into the house. There were also big black widow spiders with their red bellies, and ugly rats and mice that found a way into the house as well.

When my mother locked me in the closet, which happened frequently, my biggest fear was that one of those rattlesnakes, black widow spiders, or fat rats would come into the closet with me. They could slither under the door (it had a gap because the door had been cut too high off the floor). Inside the closet, I sat on top of the laundry basket, where the dirty laundry was kept, and pulled my legs and arms in tight, hoping if one of those vile and dangerous creatures did get in, it could not easily touch me. Even so, I knew they could get into the basket.

My mother didn't wash clothes very often because the washing machine was outdoors by the side of the house, and it was hand operated. My father had to fill it with water from the well that had been heated on the stove. My mother washed the clothes by hand in the barrel of it, and then she had to turn a handle that caused the two rollers to wring each piece out. In the deep-freezing, snowy winters in Wyoming, that process didn't happen at all. Looking back now, I can't imagine how we survived it. But at the time, I was a young child and so engulfed in my own fear that I couldn't think about much else.

The outhouse—something we had to use because we had no inside plumbing—was a ways from the house, and far too often a black widow spider was sitting in the center of a web it had formed over the opening of the wooden toilet seat. It was frightening beyond words, and my mother seldom wanted to walk with me there or help me in any way. Her irritation toward me whenever I ran back to the house to tell her that a scary spider was over the toilet seat again was made very clear to me. For that meant she would have to come out with a rolled up newspaper and light it on fire in order to burn the spider up before dropping it in the horrible abyss below. Our toilet paper was pages from catalogs that came in the mail because there was no money for real toilet paper. It was too much of a luxury.

From as far back in my childhood as I can recall, I remember being afraid of my mother and her erratic and threatening behavior. I was also afraid of the extreme and bitter cold, the dangerous rattlesnakes, black widow spiders, and rats. Because we were very poor, I often went to bed hungry. When you are starving, and there is no food in the house, and no way to buy any because there isn't any money with which to buy it, it is frightening—especially as a child. I didn't know if one day there would never be any more. All that established a habit of fear in me.

Before I started school in the first grade—there was no kinder-garten—I came down with diphtheria and nearly died. I didn't really know what it meant to die except that I wouldn't be in pain any-more. I had been in agony with this terrible sickness long enough that dying actually sounded good to me. Diphtheria is a horrible disease, and there was no vaccine for it at that time. At least that's what I was told. My mother believed that doctors—among many other people—were out to kill her, so she would never go to one unless she was forced to. Thank God a neighbor from the nearest farm miles away came to see if we were okay after a terrible blizzard and discovered we were snowed in and I was deathly sick. He drove us to the nearest hospital 20 miles away, where the doctor there took tests to find out what was wrong with me. In the meantime, until he got the test results back, he gave me medicine that unfortunately didn't help at all.

When the test results came back, this good, kind, and merciful doctor found out I had diphtheria and drove the 20 miles from the hospital to try to find our house in yet another blizzard. When he couldn't go any farther in his car, he walked to a neighboring farm-house and got directions to our house from the people there. He walked miles across fields in the snow to get to us. I still remember hearing him knock at our back door as I was trying to sleep on a cot near the potbellied stove to keep warm. He came in from the cold and told us I had diphtheria. He gave me a shot, and within hours I began to feel better enough to swallow some liquid. I had not been able to eat or drink much of anything the entire time I was sick.

I still felt very weak from the diphtheria by the time I started school. The school was 20 miles away, and I was put on a bus to someplace where I didn't know anyone. I had no preparation for how loud and wild the other children were, so I was very afraid of them. I was easy prey for bullies—especially a gang of boys who terrified me and they knew it. I had lost so much weight that I was teased mercilessly by the children about being too skinny. In that place and time, "too skinny" was not considered attractive. Once at school, I only felt safe in the classroom. It was calm and peaceful, and I loved learning to read and write. I always found solace in books, and it would be that way for the rest of my life. Reading and writing was how I survived my life.

As I grew up, all the fear I had as a child never went away. For one thing, my mother only got worse. She became more violent and terrifying to me. Because her mental illness went entirely untreated, it progressed downhill. She could always pull herself together in front of other people, but only for a short time.

The older I got, the more serious my anxiety, panic attacks, and depression became. After I left home to work and put myself through college, I had a fear of failure that caused me to labor extremely hard at whatever jobs I had in order to support myself and have a secure place to live. I knew I had to be educated and develop skills so I would never live paycheck to paycheck without ever getting ahead, like my parents had. I took out a student loan for only one semester at college and immediately saw the futility of being in that kind of debt. I feared I would never get out from under it. It was not a burden I wanted to carry, so I worked nights, weekends, and summers to get enough money to make it through each semester. Behind all the hard work was always the fear of failure and the possible consequences of that. Failure was not an option for me, because going back to live in an apartment with my mother was definitely not an option either.

Fear overwhelmed me and controlled my life. And I made poor choices because of it.

Fear Can Get into Our Head and Under Our Skin

None of us gets away without experiencing struggle, suffering, or loss in our life. We fear those times, but we can begin right now to overcome those fears by saying, "God has not given me a spirit of fear." A spirit of fear controls us. I am not talking about when you feel afraid *about* something, which could be a prompting from the Holy Spirit to warn you to go another way or check the lock on your door. I am talking about a real spirit of fear. You know it when you have it because you feel it. It crawls up your back like a cold wet blanket and stays there because you cannot shake it off.

When I was in high school, I could never risk bringing any-one home because of my mother. However, I did develop a close friendship with a girl in my grade who took the same drama classes I did. We were in the school plays together, so we spent a lot of time rehearsing and conversing. We were kindred spirits and able to share more of our past with each other than either of us had ever before communicated to anyone. Her experience was very similar to what I experienced with my mentally ill mother, only her mother was an alcoholic. The particulars and differences in our mothers' problems notwithstanding, the consequences for each of us were almost the same. She couldn't bring anyone home to her house either. One day I went with her to her house after school in order to pick up her copy of the play we were doing so we could rehearse, and we found her mother drunk on the floor. She had warned me that might hap-pen. We left quickly.

When our mothers would slip into their own self-focused worlds and have crazy episodes, it made us feel abandoned and rejected. We each recognized that our mother was not there for us physically, mentally, or emotionally. We were both grateful to find a friend who completely understood the issues and with whom we could share this enormous hidden part of our lives.

The meaner and more horrible our mothers were, the more our fathers tried to downplay their behavior. Both of our fathers seemed to think that our mother's treatment of us was no big deal. *They* tolerated it, so surely *we* could too. In fact, whenever I went to my father for help, he said, "Just ignore her."

"I can't, Dad," I responded to him as a teenager. "I have been *raised* with her insanity. You never even met her until you were in your thirties. You were already formed as an adult and had a choice. I had no choice about being terrorized and tortured by her violence and insanity."

My friend's father told her nearly the same thing. Our fathers were no help, except that their very presence surely kept us from being destroyed by our mothers.

My mother told me repeatedly, "I didn't have that, why should you?" "I didn't have more than one cheap pair of shoes a year, why should you?" Never mind that I had not only grown out of them, but the soles had come loose and had to be glued on every day. She was furious when I wanted to go to college and said, "I didn't get to go to college, why should you?" My mother's father believed it was a waste of money to educate a woman because she was just going to get married and have babies anyway, and her education would be a waste of time and money. It was a common thought among poor people coming out of the Great Depression when money was so hard to come by. Many in that generation were afraid their whole lives of the possibility that it could all happen again. Who could blame them?

In our twenties, after going to separate universities, my friend and I met up in Hollywood, where we had both found work, and we shared an apartment. By that time our fears manifested in different ways. I became plagued with depression and anxiety, and she became multiphobic. When I was 28, after going through drugs, the occult, Eastern religions, and bad relationships, I received the Lord. That is when *my* life began to happen. But *she* developed agoraphobia, which meant she was afraid to leave her house, even to go to the grocery store. We were living in separate houses by then. In trying to help her with this, she let me tell her about my experience receiving the Lord and how much freedom from fear and anxiety I had found. She could see my experience was real and I had been changed by it. I led her to the Lord, and she let me take her to my church. After that, I prayed with her almost daily and encouraged her to seriously read the Bible I gave her. Gradually, that incapacitating fear quieted down enough for her to drive herself to church. This was an amazing breakthrough.

The frightening situations my friend and I experienced as children became etched in our mind until even though the things we feared no longer posed any direct threat, we still behaved as though they did. It seems that the more terrifying our memories, and the younger we experience them, the more deeply they are engraved in our mind and heart and the harder they are to get over.

When traumatic things happen to us, the memories of them play over and over in our head like a continuous loop tape. And that is especially so if the most important person in our life at the time is the one who caused the trauma. These experiences get into our mind and under our skin so that we feel the fear over and over and we develop a constant feeling of insecurity and impending doom.

When that happens, fear grabs ahold of our emotions and begins to control our life.

Fear Can Become an Obsession

Have you ever looked up the word "phobia"? It is shocking. There are endless examples of specific fears that become irrational when they find a permanent place in someone's mind. They can appear to become part of the person and control their lives.

When we are extremely and traumatically afraid—especially if there is no one to talk us down from the ledge and walk us through the irrational part of it—we can become phobic. That means we experience extreme fear even when the source of our fear is no longer there. And one irrational fear or phobia can lead to another. This endless dysfunctional cycle opens us to the "spirit of fear" mentioned profoundly in the Bible.

I went through all those stages until I was so controlled by a spirit of fear that I couldn't escape. I didn't understand at the time that all these fears were related to being locked in a closet and abused and vulnerable to whatever danger came into the closet to harm me. I was trying to forget all that and put the past behind me, but it followed me everywhere. All I knew was that I was stuck. Trapped. And I couldn't escape.

I had a terrifying fear of the dark (achluophobia), a fear of heights (acrophobia), a fear of confined spaces (claustrophobia), a fear of being locked in an enclosed place (cleithrophobia), a fear of flying (aviophobia), a fear of snakes (ophidiophobia), a fear of knives (aichmophobia), and specifically being stabbed with a knife (sabresmittenophobia). At one point, I had a fear of insanity (agateophobia). I was afraid of becoming like my mother, because I thought, *If I can never get free of her, maybe I could wind up in her insane world.*

Even as a Christian, I had a fear of being forgotten (athazago-raphobia) that persisted for a few years after I received the Lord. I feared I was so insignificant that I could die and the Lord wouldn't notice or remember to take me to heaven. It was a genuine dread until my walk with God grew deeper and I came to know Him better. Once I had read enough of His Word and experienced enough of His love and power to convince me that His forgetting me was an impossibility, one by one these fears fell away, and I gradually became whole. (I will explain more later about how the Lord cannot forget us—ever.)

Many people fear *losing control* over their lives. They are afraid they will be sucked into something they don't like and have no way of escape. *Risk* scares people. So does *confrontation*. Most people welcome sleep because it's our escape and time to renew. For others who are phobic, even sleep frightens them. The fear of sleep, or somniphobia, causes them to feel that they could lose control and never wake up, or that bad things could happen while they are asleep and they would be unable to prevent it.

Many people develop a fear of the darkness (achluphobia), and often an accompanying condition, the fear of the bogeyman (bogyphobia). There is a fear of being ridiculed (catagelophobia), which no one wants to experience, but many people will do extreme things to avoid that risk. There is a fear of atomic explosions (atomosophobia), and who doesn't have that? But for most people, it doesn't affect their daily life.

When I was young, before I came to the Lord, I would wake up in the middle of the night with an imaginary burning sensation on my face, fearing an atomic bomb had been dropped on us. That's because my schoolmates and I were trained in school to hide from bomb explosions under our desks. Of course, once we later saw the documentaries of the results of such bombings and the way people were burned, it confirmed our suspicions that our desks would have done absolutely nothing to protect us.

My mother had a fear of throwing things out (disposophobia). She was a hoarder—but nothing like the hoarders who are chronicled on television. You wouldn't know my mother was a hoarder unless you opened up her closets, garage, or storage shed—which were all piled high to the ceiling. She was afraid she would need these things again and couldn't get them. However, she'd kept and saved so much stuff that it was all rendered totally useless.

Quite a few people of my mother's era did the same thing, but most people don't want to live with useless clutter that does no one any good. They feel better when they clean things out and give the excess away or sell it. They feel freer and lighter, less burdened, and even healthier when they get rid of things they are not using that other people need. People who have destructive fear hang on to useless things to their own detriment.

As I read more about phobias, I found a few interesting ones I did *not* have that made me feel better about the ones with which I had struggled. For example, there is a fear of books (bibliophobia), a fear of sitting (cathisophobia), a fear of colors (chromophobia), a fear of numbers (arithmophobia), a fear of flutes—yes, I said flutes (aulophobia). There is also the fear of France (francophobia), the fear of chins (geniophobia), fear of things to the left of the body (levophobia), the fear of string (linonophobia), and a fear of Walloons (walloonphobia). It's actually comforting to know that these fears never even entered my mind.

It is possible to be afraid of anything, as the large list of phobias proves. In fact there is a phobia called the fear of everything (panophobia). How miserable and bound must a person be who experiences that. I have also read about the fear of thinking (phronemophobia).

I believe I may have known a few people like that in my past. That definitely wasn't me. If anything, I could be accused of overthinking everything. Not being able to shut my mind off—especially when I needed to sleep—was a serious problem for me.

I'm sure there are reasons for all those fears, even though I cannot imagine what they would be. And I am not making light of other people's fears, believe me, because I had so many of my own that I'm certain other people couldn't understand. Even though many people have some fears in common, our fears are as individual as the things we each have experienced in life. The reason they *stay* with us so long is because we don't know what the real truth is—that is what God and His Word says about them. A huge part of getting rid of our fears is having the transforming *love* of God *in* us, inviting Him and His power to work *through* us, and then enjoying the sound mind He gives us.

Fear Can Turn into "What if?" Thoughts and Make Life Miserable

In getting rid of our fears, we have to get rid of "What if?" thoughts that can drive us crazy. They do not promote the sound mind God has for us.

Much of our fear comes from unresolved "What if?" thoughts. "What if I fail?" "What if I don't make it?" "What if I'm permanently injured?" "What if I don't recover from this disease?" "What if something bad happens to one of my children?" "What if I never find someone to marry?" "What if my marriage ends in divorce?" "What if I can't get over this problem?" "What if I can't do what I need to do?" "What if I am left all alone?" "What if I don't have enough to eat?"

"What if?" syndrome can be incapacitating and make life seem out of control. We have to recognize that we don't have to control everything ourselves. We can't do that, anyway. What we *can* do is ask *God* to be in control of our life. We can learn what God's Word says about fear and stand on His truth and promises that set us free of fear's life-diminishing stranglehold. And we must do that in order to move into all God has for us.

Just as a strong fear of being sick can actually make us sick, "What if?" thoughts can drive us crazy. There has to come a time when we rise up and say to our fears, "Stop!" And then take every fear we have to the Lord and ask Him to be in control of our life..

"What if?" fears can keep us from doing what we need to do. I'm not saying that we can't serve God if we have any fear. Most of us would never do anything if that were the case. Every great leader of the Bible had fear about something. And many of them had fear about the very thing God was calling them to do—from Adam, who was afraid in the Garden of Eden, to Jesus, who experienced fear at the prospect of enduring the torture of the cross.

King David prayed for deliverance from adversity saying, "*The troubles of my heart have enlarged*; bring me out of my distresses!" (Psalm 25:17). He also said when he was hiding in a cave from his enemy, "My spirit is overwhelmed within me; *my heart within me is distressed*" (Psalm 143:4). Have you ever felt that way? I felt exactly like that before I came to know the Lord and His love and power.

Even Moses was afraid he couldn't speak well enough to confront Pharaoh as God was calling him to do. "Moses said to the LORD, 'O my Lord, I am not eloquent, neither before nor since You have spoken to Your servant; but I am slow of speech and slow of tongue.' So the LORD said to him, 'Who has made man's mouth? Or who makes the mute, the deaf, the seeing, or the blind? Have not I, the LORD? Now *therefore, go, and I will be with your mouth and teach you what you shall say*.' But he said, 'O my Lord, please send by the hand of whomever else You may send'" (Exodus 4:10-13).

Even though God gave Moses the ability to do what He called him to do, he was still afraid and insisted that God get someone else to speak. His *fear* was greater than his *faith* in God's ability to perform miracles through him—even though God had done miracles right in front of him.

Fear of any kind can take over our life and control us. And that's the way the enemy of our soul wants it. And we allow it. All because we don't know the truth that sets us free.

As you are well aware, there are people in the world dedicated to serving the enemy of our soul by forcing fear into the hearts of people with their horrible acts. Jesus' disciples feared often, but their love of Him and their close walk with Him inspired them to face the source of their fear. And God was with them.

God is with us too. As long as we are with Him.

Fear Can Lead Us to Freedom Once We See the Truth

It's hard for me to imagine having an upbringing and a past so idyllic that a person would never be fearful of anything. It seems that every place and time has had its own frightening and dangerous conditions. This is just the nature of a fallen world that rebels against God and His ways. In today's world, where information spreads instantly, we can be aware of every problem there is. And some of us have "problem overload" so badly that we don't even want to hear or see the news. And maybe that's not a bad idea. Perhaps it's better to know enough to be able to pray about it, but know more of the Word of God by spending time reading or hearing it. With our prayers and our knowledge of God's Word, we can limit the far-reaching effects of constant bad news.

I've never seen fear so widespread and prevalent in people before in my lifetime. And this is true even among those who never seemed to be fearful persons before this. People I don't even know that well have responded to my question, "How are you doing?" with, "I am so afraid." When I ask them what they are afraid of exactly, they give me a variety of answers. For some it's personal problems. For others it's the spread of evil and violence. Still others are afraid of financial disaster and the shaky economy in their country. Many are afraid of horrible diseases and being incapacitated by them. Whatever the fear, people all over the world say the same things. I see a contagious quality about a spirit of fear that can infect many people, almost like a group fear.

A spirit of heaviness is the perfect description of depression. King David said, *"Reproach has broken my heart, and I am full of heaviness;* I looked for someone to take pity, but there was none; and for comforters, but I found none"* (Psalm 69:20). Reproach is rejection. Another psalmist said, *"My soul melts from heaviness; strengthen me according to Your word"* (Psalm 119:28).

The ultimate consequence of fear is illustrated in the Bible where it talks about *"men's hearts failing them from fear* and the expectation of those things which are coming on the earth, for the powers of heaven will be shaken"* (Luke 21:26). Just expecting bad things to happen can put us in danger of heart failure.

It's no secret that fear can kill us. That's why we need to take our fears seriously and know what steps to take in order to be rid of them. Fear makes us weak. "Do not fear; Zion, let not your hands be weak" (Zephaniah 3:16). Fear that grips us and is sustained indefinitely can weaken *our* heart muscle as well.

It's not necessarily *what* we fear, but *what we allow to overtake us.* For example, when we have a fear of snakes so extreme that we obsess over them and imagine every possible encounter with a snake so that it sends chills up our spine at the mere thought of them— even when there is no immediate threat—that depletes us. The fear

of them becomes a spirit of fear crawling up your back and grip-
ping you to the point that you are paralyzed from fright. This limits
your life and makes you weak. It messes with your mind and makes
it unstable. But God can give us freedom from all that.

Whenever you hear "What if?" words echoing in your head
regarding the things you fear most, face your fear right away by
praying about that specifically. For example, if you think as I did,
What if I trip and fall down when I walk up on the platform? don't
leave it to chance. Perhaps it came to your mind for a reason. Don't
let it become an entrenched fear from the enemy, but don't ignore
it either. Recognize that when you walk with the Lord, you are
dependent upon Him in every way. Pray, "Lord, help me to walk
on solid ground as I go up the steps to the platform. Keep me from
stumbling. Take away all panic and fear. Give me a calm mind and
a peaceful spirit."

Praying about everything that makes you afraid is the next big step
to getting free from it.

Good counseling is very helpful for uncontrollable fear, but what
can set us completely free is the truth that comes from God. He
says that a spirit of fear like that does not come from Him. He has,
instead, given us His *power*, and His *love*, and a *sound mind*. Which
leads me to believe that a mind overcome with fear is not sound. In
fact, the more fear controls us, the crazier we get. God wants each
one of us to receive the sound mind He has for us. In order to do
that, we have to fully believe what He says and stand firm on a foundation of His promises. We have to say over and over whenever we
feel that kind of overwhelming fear, "*God has not given us a spirit of*
fear, but of power and of love and of a sound mind" (2 Timothy 1:7).
Do this as often and as loud as you can until you believe it a hun-
dred percent without a doubt.

Reading the truth, *believing* the truth, *speaking* the truth, and *praying* for God's truth to liberate you will set you free. That is what I pray for you.

The ultimate consequence of unbridled fear is death. It can stop our heart if we are weak enough and frightened enough. We don't ever have to let it get that far. The reason you don't have to live in fear is because when you receive God's Son, Jesus, you are God's child, and you have an inheritance from Him. Part of your inheritance is a sound mind.

The Bible says of those who receive Jesus, "The Spirit Himself bears witness with our spirit that *we are children of God*, and if children, then heirs—*heirs of God and joint heirs with Christ*" (Romans 8:16-17).

I know too many instances where a parent left an inheritance unequally to their children. It all went to one and not the others. Or one was left out and the others received it. This control to punish a child after the parent is in the grave is hurtful for the rest of their lives. Just as bad are parents who have children but never write out a will at all, as if they themselves will never die and who cares what happens to the children afterward and what kind of uncertainty they will have to deal with after their parent is gone. Thank God that *He* never does that. We have an inheritance from Him that we share with His firstborn Son. And if we receive Him into our heart, it's a done deal.

No matter what you have been through to make you fearful, you have a way out of fear. You don't have to live a tortured life and be limited by your fears, but *you must first focus on the source of your liberation and not the source of your fears.* It is good to recognize your fears and face them by examining each one to see where it is coming from.

You may not have life-controlling fears like I had, but in your everyday life you may see or hear something that makes you afraid enough to affect your sleep, strength, health, work, relationships, or decision making. When that happens, ask God to show you any fear in you from which He can set you free. God wants you to come to Him in prayer and in His Word so He can give you His peace that passes all understanding. Who doesn't need that?

The opposite of being fearful is being bold, courageous, audacious, unafraid, brave, fearless, confident, composed, or assured. We often do our best to appear to others as these words describe while covering up the underlying fear we have in our heart. Don't let that happen to you.

Do not let fear control your life. Do what God says to be rid of it. Deliberately turn to the One who loves you more than you love yourself, and invite His love, peace, and joy to fill you. It can change everything.

Prayer Power

Lord, I ask You to reveal any fear I have that is affecting my life negatively so I can be free of it. The only fear I accept is that which You allow to wake me up to what You want me to understand. If I have given a place in my heart to fear, I confess it to You as sin because it reveals my lack of faith in You and Your Word to protect me. Forgive me and help me to stand strong against fear so I can be set completely free.

I know You will never give me a spirit of fear because that will affect and limit my life. Thank You that You have given me Your unconditional and perfect love that casts out all fear (1 John 4:18). Help me to open up and receive the full measure of Your love and also the fullness of Your Spirit of love in my heart for others.

Thank You that You have given me access to Your power through Your Holy Spirit, which enables me to live the life You have for me. Teach me to claim the clear and sound mind You have given me so I can stand strong against any error of thinking or instability in my mind.

Help me to never give place to irrational fear or allow it to occupy my mind or my life in any way. Show me where fear in me has brought about illness or infirmity of any kind so I can be healed. Keep my heart strong so that it never fails because of fear. Thank You that You are far greater than anything I fear.

In Jesus' name I pray.

WORD POWER

If you abide in My word, you are My disciples indeed.
And you shall know the truth,
and the truth shall make you free.

JOHN 8:31-32

The LORD is my light and my salvation; whom shall I fear?
The LORD is the strength of my life; of whom shall I be afraid?

PSALM 27:1

Say to those who are fearful-hearted, "Be strong, do not fear!
Behold, your God will come with vengeance,
with the recompense of God;
He will come and save you."

ISAIAH 35:4

Why are you cast down, O my soul?
And why are you disquieted within me?
Hope in God, for I shall yet praise Him
for the help of His countenance.

PSALM 42:5

Wait on the LORD; be of good courage,
and He shall strengthen your heart;
wait, I say, on the LORD!

PSALM 27:14

2

What Do We Fear Most?

Most people are often afraid of far more than they openly reveal. And they may fear different things at different times. We all are afraid of anything that is dangerous or painful or in any way poses a threat to our well-being. And not just a threat to ourselves, but also to those we care about and love. There are some common basic fears many people have, and it's good to recognize what they are and see if we struggle with anything like them. It is also good to face those fears with God and His truth. Below are a few of them.

The Fear of Small, Dark Places and the Creepy Things in Them

Have you, or someone you know, ever been terrified of being shut in a small, dark place with the possibility of creepy, crawly creatures or persons being in there with you? Or have you ever freaked out when a spider crawled across the floor near you or across your arm? Have you ever screamed with terror and had someone come running in to see what evil person was threatening you, and from the high perch where you were standing you pointed out the scary spider and screamed, "There!" And they looked in that direction with a blank stare and said, "Where?" You are terrified, as though your life is threatened. And all they see is a spider. You are horrified, and the person with you is trying to figure out why. They calmly kill it, and you are still perched on your couch or chair, and you pray they don't come near you with the mangled carcass. I personally relate to that more than I care to describe. I had such a fear of small, dark places and the creepy things that might be in there with me that it affected me profoundly. I know it was because I was frequently locked in that small, dark closet by my mother and feared spiders and snakes could be in there too.

I didn't get free of that fear until I received the Lord. But before that I tried to do it on my own. I tried to liberate myself from the tremendous fear and anxiety that was ruining my life, so I sought the help of a highly recommended psychologist. He asked me to describe in detail the closet I was locked up in under the stairs in that old stone ranch house. He said that describing the source of fear can often make it less menacing. I found that to be helpful, but I still did not get free of the fear associated with that entire experience.

While I was in therapy with this doctor, he told me that going back to look at something that frightens you can make it not appear as threatening as you remembered it to be. So I decided to travel back to Wyoming to visit that old ranch. Two of my extended family members knew exactly where it was, and so I flew to their town and they drove me to the ranch house. It was exactly as I remembered it. I knew the layout of the property—including the blacksmith shop, the chicken coop, the corral for the horses, the field for the cows, and the shed for storing farm equipment. And I knew every detail of the small stone ranch house. Nothing had changed at all. It had been abandoned, and it looked as though no one had lived there for many years, if at all, after we left. My family members had heard that the valley it was in was going to be made into a reservoir, and it would be totally underwater soon. I was grateful we visited there before that happened.

I found an open window and crawled inside the kitchen— ignoring my family member's warnings not to do so since we were on private property and could still get arrested or shot by the own- ers if they should come upon us. I told them I had to see that closet, and I couldn't come this far without doing so. They stayed out- side. Once I was inside, I knew every bit of the layout of the house, but it was even smaller than I remembered. I immediately saw the closet under the stairs between the kitchen and the living room and opened the door to look inside.

Everything in the closet was covered with dust and spider webs. It smelled musty and old. I was still afraid I would find a rattlesnake or some black widow spiders in the countless webs, so I did not enter the closet at all. Among the cobwebs were old random boards and worthless junk. Of course, I didn't touch any of it, but I was struck by how tiny the closet was.

I didn't go up the stairs because the two tiny bedrooms upstairs were always very cramped and uninviting. I had no interest in see- ing them even if I would have had the time to do so.

On the hearth of the stone fireplace in the tiny living room was my mother's old heavy iron. I remembered how she would put that on top of the black wood-burning stove in the kitchen until it was hot enough to iron a piece of clothing. That didn't happen very often unless we were going to town for groceries, and she would iron something to wear.

I remembered how driving out from that place was a major trek up the mountain on a rocky dirt road. We had to first cross the creek in back of our house in order to get up the hill to the main road. Sometimes, when the creek rose after a rain, the water was too high to forge across. When our old truck couldn't make it over the creek, we had to ride our horse, Bessie, up the steep hill to the road in order to get the mail.

All those memories came back instantly like a flood. But the closet didn't look nearly as menacing as it once had appeared to me when I was a child and locked up in it. That helped to ease my fears but didn't get rid of them completely. I was missing a very important aspect of true freedom. The truth.

If there have been dark and frightening places, events, or memories in your life, sometimes going back to see them again with a new perspective of being a survivor can help you to overcome them. Sometimes there are dark places *within us* that we are hesitant to look into for fear of what we will find there. Whatever it is, we need the truth and the love of God to enable us to get completely free.

The Fear of Evil Around Us and Feeling Powerless

As a child, I had no control over anything in my life. I believe the feeling of having no control over the things we fear is a big part of being tortured by them. My tremendous fear of flying was so strong for that reason—having absolutely no control over any part of it. It was like huddling under a desk in grade school for protection from an atomic bomb if it was dropped on us. I think I always knew how pointless that was.

We all fear the evil around us in our world and how out of control and dangerous it is. Often the evil we fear most can be seen right on our television—sometimes as it occurs—whether someplace else in the world or closer to our own home. The weapons available to the purveyors of evil and fear are growing more frightening every day.

And the reason evil people do these kinds of things is because they know it weakens us mentally, emotionally, and physically.

Who can feel safe when so many weapons of mass destruction are available to be delivered to where we live if someone desires to do so and is crazy enough to do it? We have had great leaders in our country who helped us not bow to fear or give in to the demands of evil, but there is only one leader who will heal our wounds and lead us into His peace that passes all understanding. The Bible says, "Why should I fear in the days of evil, when the iniquity at my heels surrounds me?" (Psalm 49:5). We have access to the greatest power in the world and peace in the midst of the worst situations. We have a God who loves us enough to help us in a big way. (More about that in the next chapter.)

The Fear of Being Insignificant, Unimportant, or Invisible

If we have been made to feel that we were disposable, inconvenient, unloved, insignificant, unimportant, not special in any way, or as if we will never amount to anything in our life, that fear looms large over us every day. That's the way I was made to feel, because some of those exact words were what I was told by my mother when I was a child.

My father told me after my mother died in her sixties that he and my mother had decided to never tell me anything nice about myself so that I would not grow up conceited or arrogant. I see how well that worked! I grew up anxious, depressed, fearful, and suicidal instead. I know that was back in the dark ages of child rearing when children were to be seen and not heard—or in my case, neither. But this idea was carried to the extreme even for that time.

I started writing my autobiography after my mother died. By that time I was married and had two young children. I had been praying for some time that God would heal her and she would one day be in her right mind and come to know Him as her deliverer, but she only got worse with each passing day. After I finished writing that book and before it was released, my husband and I and our children drove to my father's small farm about four hours north of Los Angeles. I needed for him to read the book and sign a personal release because he was in the book in a big way, and he might think of it as an invasion of his privacy. While the names of other people were deliberately changed in the book to protect their privacy, he would be identified, and I wanted to make sure he was okay with that.

I knew some parts of the book were going to be very rough for him to read. He was going to find out for the first time some of the terrible things I had done in my life, and I feared his reaction to all that. Even though I wrote a great deal about my mother's abuse, I certainly didn't tell everything. And I hoped he would see that.

After the rest of us went to bed that evening, he stayed up all night reading the book. When I got up in the morning, he was still sitting in his recliner in the den, looking out the window deep in thought. I dreaded what he might say and wondered if he would even sign the release. But when I asked for his reaction to reading the book, his only words were, "Well, you made your mother look good."

I was beyond grateful to him for that. It meant that he not only saw how terrible my mother was, but he recognized how much I had withheld in the book because I knew people could not bear to read about all that. He told me he had thought she was only that abusive to *him*. He didn't know about the closet—at least not to the extent she used it to punish me. One of my aunts later told me that my father said to her regarding me and my autobiography, "She didn't tell the half of it." He recognized the truth. My aunt knew that too, because my mother had done some of the same things to her when she was a child, after their own mother died and my mother baby-sat her.

All that early abuse from my mother caused me to be filled with anxiety and fear that I would never amount to anything. I felt that no matter what I accomplished in my life, it would never be enough to please anyone. Suicidal thoughts plagued me every day, and I even attempted suicide once when I was 14. Because of my mother's fear that people were out to kill her, she switched her bottles of pain pills and sleeping pills with other pills that weren't as dangerous. These pills had been prescribed for her when my sister was born. I didn't take enough of the right pills to do the job. So instead of ending my miserable life as I'd hoped, the pills just made me very sick. My mother's craziness actually saved my life. Who knew?

Fourteen years after that suicide attempt, and having tried every way I knew to reach God and find a reason to live, I was once again on the brink of gathering enough sleeping pills to end my life. Only this time I was 28 years old and knew how to do the job right. I had never told anyone about my experience with my mother, except my friend in high school who I mentioned in the first chapter, because it was too humiliating. I always feared others would suspect I might become mentally ill like her. Back then, mental illness was a well-kept secret in families. It was not understood or accepted in any way. Letting anyone know was too risky. Besides, I had tried everything I knew of to get free of my depression, anxiety, and fear, and nothing had worked. I couldn't live with that horrible emotional pain anymore.

It was during the time I was planning my suicide that my friend Terry, a singer I had been working with on television, saw my state of mind. During a recording session one day, she said, "I can see you are not doing well. Why don't you come with me to meet my pastor?

I know he can help you." I knew she was a Christian because she'd told me about her church and her pastor and how the Lord had affected her life. I'd met her parents when she and I were working on live television shows in Hollywood. They attended each one and always seemed to be normal, nice, kind, and caring people.

Of course God can help her, I thought. *She came from a normal family. She isn't an emotionally damaged person like I am. She isn't hopeless. She has everything to live for. She doesn't have crippling anxiety and incapacitating depression. She has never feared in her life that she could die of starvation or end up homeless, or, even worse, that she might have to go back and live with an insane mother.*

Even though my sister was still living at home at the time, I felt it was better for her if I wasn't there because of the intense friction between me and my mother. My mother's irrational screaming at me couldn't be good for my sister, who was 12 years younger. And it seemed that while my mother attacked me violently, she wasn't that way with my sister. My mother was neglectful with her, and I think all that contributed to my sister's feelings of abandonment years later. Also, I had to live away from home because my depression and anxiety became so much worse when I was around my mother for even a few minutes. It always took weeks for me to recover from that.

I know some people can be so desperate to be recognized as having value, significance, or purpose that they will do anything to make it happen. Even being known for something bad is deemed better by some emotionally damaged people than not being acknowledged at all.

This was made plain to me when I went to speak at a women's prison after my autobiography came out. The chaplain there believed my story could help the many women who had been emotionally damaged in their childhood. After I told my personal story of brokenness, anxiety, panic, depression, and fear to the women at the prison—and how God took all that away and healed me—there was not a dry eye in the group. Many were even sobbing so uncontrollably that the guards came in with Kleenex and gave it to them. God was knocking on the door of their heart as they were finally able to recognize His love for them.

One young girl in particular, who couldn't have been older than her early twenties, asked to speak to me privately. The chaplain arranged a meeting between us in a private room. She told me she was in prison because she had killed her baby by smothering him. She had been badly abused all her life by her mother and stepfather. When they found out she was pregnant in her teens, they threw her out of the house. She had no money and no home. She found a temporary place to stay while she was pregnant, but shortly after the baby was born she was pushed out on her own again, only this time with a baby.

Looking back, it was easy to see that the young mother should have given the baby up for adoption, but no one was there to help her do that. So when the baby was still only a few months old, the girl didn't know how to handle the baby's crying. She had the emotional maturity of a child herself, so she couldn't handle the responsibility of having a child. She had no one to help her cope. One night when the baby was crying and she couldn't get him to stop, she put a pillow over his head and smothered him. I am so sorry if this hurts your heart to read about it as much as it hurts mine to write it, but I just want to make this one point. She told me that once she was arrested for the murder of her child and taken to jail, as she was being photographed by news photographers and was the center of attention during her trial and all that led up to it, she said to herself, "Now I *am* somebody."

A deep chill ran through me, and my heart broke for that baby and also for the young mother. To be that deprived of love and encouragement to the point that no matter what heinous and unthinkable thing she had done, it was better than feeling she was the insignificant waste of humanity her mother and stepfather had made her feel she was. It shocked me to my core to hear that.

I told the young woman that only Jesus can forgive us of all our terrible mistakes, and only He can truly give us worth and a sense of purpose. I told her she had value in His eyes and He still loved her, and He had a purpose for her if she would surrender her life to Him. I assured her that He could transform her and give her a life of significance. She did receive the Lord, and I prayed she would fully repent and know God's forgiveness and be restored to a life of purpose, which God has for everyone—even behind bars.

That story illustrates the extreme consequences of feeling worthless, disposable, unloved, and insignificant. Many people fear this more than anything. If you have trouble believing a person could actually feel that way after an unthinkable act such as that, it's because you have never been made to feel that badly in a serious and ongoing manner. Believe me, emotional damage like that is real.

In contrast to this young woman, I was so convinced that I was worthless and unloved and could never amount to anything significant that I couldn't see any way out of my life other than to destroy myself. This is why too many young kids are killing themselves. We have all seen this in the news, or with people we know, or perhaps it has happened to you. A child's suicide is one of the most heartbreaking things that can happen to a parent. The guilt is a bottomless pit, and only God can pull a parent out of it.

I know of kids who are repeatedly bullied with no one coming to their defense. They feel hopeless, hated, worthless, lonely, withdrawn, and filled with fear, and they cannot see any way out of that.

They feel isolated because they are embarrassed to tell anyone what is going on. And some have been threatened with worse treatment if they do tell someone. But God can change all that for them. And our prayers for them can make a major difference. That's why we must pray for every child to have God's love in their life and people around them who can model it in a way that pleases Him.

If you have ever had the fear of being insignificant, worthless, or purposeless, know that God does not, never has, and never will see you that way. Because you are God's son or daughter, He loves you as much as He loves anyone else. "Behold what manner of love the Father has bestowed on us, that we should be called children of God!" (1 John 3:1). The Bible says, "If our heart condemns us, God is greater than our heart, and knows all things" (1 John 3:20). That means although you may beat yourself up because you believe you are insignificant or worth nothing, God knows the real truth about you—that you have been gifted by Him and have a high calling and purpose. You have been made to believe lies about yourself, and He wants you to know the truth.

Other people can make us feel invisible, unseen, unnoticed, and unappreciated. But God never does. The way to combat the fear of being insignificant or unimportant is to understand that God will never make you feel that way. In fact, quite the opposite. He sent His Son, Jesus, to lay down His life for *you*, so you can have a better life now and a perfect life with Him for eternity. (More about that in chapter 3.)

The Fear of Man and the Fear of Rejection

Another fear common among many people, and closely related to fear of insignificance, is the fear of man. *"The fear of man brings a snare, but whoever trusts in the LORD shall be safe"* (Proverbs 29:25).

Fearing what people think of us has a lot to do with what we think about ourselves. The Bible says we are not to have any fear of man because it controls our life and keeps us weak. A man-pleasing spirit is not productive; a God-fearing person is liberated from that.

We all want to feel accepted. None of us wants to appear repulsive or offensive to anyone. But it is impossible to please everyone. Pleasing *God* has to be our greatest desire. We do that by loving Him and having faith in Him and His Word. He says in His Word that everything not done from faith is sin and does not please Him. So doubt is a sin. God says, *"The just shall live by faith*; but if anyone draws back, my soul has no pleasure in him" (Hebrews 10:38). Knowing God's will and living with strong faith in Him is the only way to live and be free of the fear of man. God says, "Listen to Me, you who know righteousness, you people in whose heart is My law: *Do not fear the reproach of men, nor be afraid of their insults"* (Isaiah 51:7).

Related to the fear of man is the fear of rejection. We can feel rejected early in childhood by a parent or later in life by bullies, cruel peers, abusive strangers, significant others, or coworkers. The possibilities for rejection are endless. We only have to be seriously and painfully rejected once for the fear of rejection to take root in us.

Our own feelings of rejection can be sensed by our children, and we need to not only pray for ourselves to be free of this, but also to intercede for each child we have that they will know the love of God, His full acceptance of them, and His pleasure in them. Don't let your child believe lies about himself or herself—especially if you have done that yourself and know firsthand how damaging that is.

Whatever damages your spirit will leave a hurt and wound so deep that without the healing and restoring love of God poured out in you, it's hard to heal from it by yourself. You need to personally know the love and acceptance God has for you. Every experience of rejection adds up to constantly feeling the fear of rejection all the time.

I felt rejected by both my parents. Even though my mother was the abuser, I wondered why my father never rescued me from her cruelty. Because my school was 20 miles away, and our nearest neighbors were miles away, I never had any friends. My parents didn't socialize with other people. I went to first grade in Wyoming, but the following year my mother left my dad, and she and I moved in with relatives in another state. That year I went to three different schools in three different cities for second grade. After my mother was asked to leave each relative's home where we had been staying, she finally ran out of relatives and came back to my dad, and I returned to my original school.

Just as no one knew me at the other schools that year, no one knew me at this same school where I had been two years before. I was invisible to them, which actually felt like a safer place to me than being noticed and bullied. By that time I was so afraid of being rejected that I didn't even try to make friends. It became clear no one was interested in me. Finally in third grade, I met a girl in class who at least knew my name. I never forgot her and have always been grateful for her kindness.

After third grade we moved to California, where I started fourth grade. We weren't isolated there, so I walked to school and was able to make some friends. People appeared far friendlier in Los Angeles because almost everyone was from somewhere else. Still, the fear of rejection moved with me wherever I went.

In Los Angeles, everyone else in my class lived in a nice neighborhood, but we were much poorer than anyone I went to school with. We lived in an old shack of a house behind a gas station. That put up a social barrier for me, and I often felt rejection because of it. I was left out of birthday parties and special events. I couldn't get there anyway because my father worked seven days a week at the gas station, and my mother was wrapped up in all the demons she entertained and the imaginary people she talked to that she thought were out to kill her. I didn't dare bring anyone home to that. She would even tell off innocent people in a store or on the street, accusing them of following her and trying to murder her. It was way too scary to think she might verbally attack the parents of one of my schoolmates in that same way.

Being rejected is bad enough, but having the *fear* of rejection with you wherever you go is brutal. It doesn't have to be that way. Ask God to show you any feelings or experiences you have had with rejection in your life. Some people who feel rejected may also reject God. They think, *Where was God when I needed Him?* The truth is, God is everywhere, but He is with us in power only when He is invited to be. We can change that when we humble ourselves before Him, repent of our selfishness, pride, and rejection of Him, and ask Him to come into our life in a powerful way. God said, "My people are destroyed for lack of knowledge" (Hosea 4:6). He rejects those who reject Him. He accepts those who receive Him. (More about that in the next chapter.)

Sometimes we reject ourselves, and that's bad in every way—especially for our mental, emotional, and physical health. When we lose confidence and gain self-hatred instead, we find it hard to forgive ourselves for never being good enough. We don't believe we have any purpose in life. That self-rejection is not of the Lord and has to go.

We are weakened and worn out by a spirit of rejection, which brings along with it feelings of being abandoned, alone, sad, and discouraged. The hopelessness and weariness are exhausting. Left unchanged, this can lead to perfectionism, and that is a form of pride, which leads to more rejection by people who don't want to be around that. We think the only way to not be rejected is to be perfect. All the things that come with rejection—such as anger, jealousy, bitterness, and resentment—can weaken us to the point of sickness.

Unforgiveness is another side effect of rejection, and it is sheer torture. It eats away at us like a cancer. Some people have a hard time forgiving those who they feel rejected them or hurt them. This produces bitterness in their heart. All kinds of physical problems and diseases can manifest in someone with bitterness and unforgiveness. When we suffer from self-rejection and have the *fear* of rejection deeply rooted in our heart, those two things will surely affect our body if we don't put a stop to it.

People who refuse to forgive will be tormented in many ways. Unforgiveness is a constant weight on our shoulders that we were not made to carry, and it wears our body down. Forgiveness is our choice to make—not based on whether we feel like doing it, but on wanting to obey God and get free of the things that will separate us from a close walk with Him. He waits for us to separate ourselves from *iniquity*. "If I regard iniquity in my heart, the Lord will not hear" (Psalm 66:18). *Unforgiveness is iniquity*, and it keeps God from hearing our prayers. It's not that He *cannot* hear them. It's that He *won't* until we get that out of our heart.

Jesus understands rejection. Isaiah prophesied that Jesus would be "despised and rejected by men, a Man of sorrows and acquainted with grief...*He was wounded for our transgressions, He was bruised for our iniquities*; the chastisement for our peace was upon Him, and *by His stripes we are healed*" (Isaiah 53:3,5).

Jesus bore rejection so we can be forever accepted by Him and made whole.

God wants us to be free of fear. The fear of man and the fear of rejection is a good place to start. Ask Him to show you if these are problems in your life, and if so, ask Him to set you free from them. He can do that.

Jesus said, "If the Son makes you free, you shall be free indeed" (John 8:36). In His presence there is healing and wholeness and restoration. And when He makes you free, you are truly free.

The Fear of Talking to People

I have actually heard people say they would rather die than get up in front of people to speak. And they seem to mean it, although I doubt they would actually follow through on that if the two choices presented themselves. Yet I certainly understand it. Even so, I have been close to death enough times in my life to know that speaking in front of people was more appealing to me than dying. Of course, the only dying that came to my mind was filled with pain and terror. Perhaps if it were merely a matter of painlessly disappearing, I might have chosen that over risking humiliation and rejection. When the brutality of reality is in your face every moment of your life, you become a realist and let go of idealistic thoughts.

Public speaking may not be one of your greatest fears, but it is for many people. The fear of delivering a message to others has a lot to do with the fear of rejection, the fear of failure, the fear of humiliation, the fear of being exposed, the fear of losing control, the fear of being criticized, the fear of all eyes on you, or the fear of your mind failing or freezing and going blank. It's more than just getting up to talk in front of a crowd. The very nature of it forces you to think about all the fears associated with it.

Getting up in front of people to speak, when they are focused entirely and specifically on you, can be extremely frightening for most people. It was for me too. Speaking has always been a challenge for me. That's what happens when you are locked in a closet for much of your early childhood and silenced because you have been shown that no one cares about anything you have to say. I was punished for crying or trying to say anything, so I learned to keep quiet. As a result, I couldn't talk very well. I didn't come out of my shell until I was in high school and participating in drama classes. There I could memorize lines and deliver them as if I were someone else. I could speak them as the character in a script, or as the person I wanted to be. At some point in each dramatic play or improvisation, in my mind I was not the person who couldn't speak.

The way I felt about speaking before people is perfectly described by the apostle Paul when he said, "My speech and my preaching were not with persuasive words of human wisdom, but in *demonstration of the Spirit and of power*, that *your faith should not be in the wisdom of men* but in the power of God" (1 Corinthians 2:4-5).

Paul did not influence people for the Lord because he was a great speaker, but because he moved in the power of God. He was not self-confident. He depended on the Holy Spirit, who is the power of God. Paul did not want anyone to be impressed with him, but rather with the power of God manifesting through him.

Speaking publicly frightened me for years because I didn't have the skills for it. But once I got rid of the fear of man and fear of rejection and started wanting to obey God and please Him, I was able to get up and tell people about what He had done for me. The only way I can do that now is by believing completely that God has called me to do it, believing in the message God has given me, and caring more about the people I'm speaking to than whether they are going to like me or not. However, whenever I get ready to speak, I still pray about each fear and "What if?" thought. In addition to that, I think about how much God loves the people I am speaking to, who have come to hear a Word from Him. I ask God to show me what *they* are going through and what *they* need.

Whenever you speak in front of people—whether it's just a few people or thousands, you need to know whether God has called you to do it or not. He may not have specifically called you to that particular message, which might have been assigned to you by the people or company you work for, or for whom you are doing this, but you are always called by God to communicate His spirit of love, joy, and peace whenever you speak to anyone about anything. People always need that message. God always wants them to have it, and He has opened the door of opportunity for you to bring it. Even if you are in a limiting situation, you can find ways to communicate God's love.

Many times in the Bible, God called someone to deliver a message to certain people, and the person called to do so was terrified of the possible consequences. That's because in certain instances they could have been killed for what they were saying. Any one of us would have been terrified in their position. But they learned to rely on God.

After I received the Lord and experienced so much miraculous emotional healing and spiritual deliverance, I began to rise above those early crippling experiences. I wrote a book about all that called *Out of Darkness*, and in it I told how all my personal attempts to get free of depression, anxiety, fear, loneliness, feelings of isolation, abandonment, and rejection always failed, and I came to the conclusion that there was no way out for me. So I planned my suicide, even though it wasn't that I wanted to die. I just didn't want to wake up with the pain anymore, and I believed at this point there was no other way to stop it.

As I mentioned earlier, while I was still in the process of collecting enough sleeping pills to do the job right and carry out my plan, my friend Terry took me to see her pastor, and I received the Lord. And this began the restoration process. It was several years of healing and deliverance and learning to walk with God and live His way and studying His Word until it became life to me.

As I grew in knowledge of the Lord, I heard God's call to my heart to speak about what He had done for me. And I was terrified. I knew how inadequate I was as a speaker. This wasn't going to be me playing a part or pretending to be someone else. This was me being me. Exposed and open. When I first started speaking, it was to small groups. I read in the Bible, "Who has despised the day of small things?" (Zechariah 4:10). I certainly didn't do that. I welcomed speaking in front of just a few people at first because I knew I was not ready for prime time. I just wanted to tell others about the miracles God had done in my life. But the crowds quickly grew bigger, and they were always overwhelming to me. However, each time I spoke I saw God speak through me.

I was so nervous the first time I got up in front of a huge crowd of people to speak on this subject that I was shaking badly and wasn't even sure if my voice would work. I felt the way David did when he was being pursued by his enemy. He said, "My heart is severely pained within me, and the terrors of death have fallen upon me. Fearfulness and trembling have come upon me, and horror has overwhelmed me. So I said, 'Oh, that I had wings like a dove! I would fly away and be at rest'" (Psalm 55:4-6).

I think I may have actually prayed those exact words. But God answered my prayers for help. And I didn't die while speaking or, worse than that, humiliate myself. It was *my* voice, but it was *His* Spirit bringing it alive to people as only He can do.

The more I confronted the fear of speaking in front of people, the freer I became. God's truth set me free. His promise is, "Do not fear, for you will not be ashamed; neither be disgraced, for you will not be put to shame" (Isaiah 54:4). It helped me most to think about how much God loved the people I was speaking to and how much *they* needed to know what He could do in their lives. I focused on them and not me.

If you have ever experienced the fear of speaking before people, or if you have that fear now, know God has freedom for you. You don't have to become a public speaker, but you do need to be able to share with others what He has done. This is an important message that could save someone's life. Ask God to set you free from that fear so you are able to hear from Him when someone needs to know the truth that can liberate *them*. Forget about yourself and focus on what God is showing you. This is the freedom He wants you to walk in.

The Fear of Unending Pain and Suffering

Simon Peter—who was with Jesus every day and *saw* who He really was and experienced His love and power—still bowed to his own fear when the time came for him to make a choice. The Lord had said to him earlier, "Simon, Simon! Indeed, Satan has asked for you, that he may sift you as wheat. But *I have prayed for you, that your faith should not fail*; and when you have returned to Me, strengthen your brethren" (Luke 22:31-32).

Peter responded to Jesus saying, "*Lord, I am ready to go with You, both to prison and to death*" (Luke 22:33). But Jesus knew the truth and said, "I tell you, Peter, the rooster shall not crow this day before you will deny three times that you know Me" (Luke 22:34). It was true. Peter's fear was far greater than his desire to admit he followed Jesus. After Jesus was captured, Peter denied Him three times just as Jesus said he would. And Peter was terribly saddened by his own failure.

If Peter—who witnessed the miracles of Jesus with his own eyes—couldn't control his fears, how can we? But Peter had not yet witnessed the greatest miracle of all—the resurrection of Jesus. And while we didn't witness the resurrection of Jesus, we have the advantage of knowing the testimonies of the many people who did see Him after He was resurrected. We have the truth about what Jesus accomplished on our behalf.

Because we witness so much unimaginable suffering in this world, it makes us fearful for ourselves and our loved ones. It's now possible for someone on the other side of the world to destroy us in the most heinous of ways. But we also know that constant, fervent prayer to the almighty God of the universe, who is more powerful than all the weapons man can come up with to obliterate his enemies, can work miracles.

Personally, I have suffered a great deal of pain in my life, and it's definitely something to be feared. Time goes by slowly when you are miserable. Every moment is elongated when you are in pain. The slow motion of suffering is not a mystery. Pain and suffering are what we all want to avoid. We will do anything to relieve the severe discomfort and brokenness of our body, emotions, or mind.

People who are arrogant in their judgment of others who are suffering are most likely people who have never truly suffered. They don't know the agony of unbearable pain so intense that they want to die when it seems to go on and on and no relief is to be found. They don't know what it is like to struggle for every breath, or not be able to do the simplest things they used to be able to do before the accident, or the incident, or the disease.

But when you have truly suffered, you are thankful for every day you don't suffer anymore. You become patient with people who do. When you suffer, you have two choices: Either you become bitter and angry against God for allowing it, or you walk with God through it, depending on Him to lead and sustain you every moment of every day. Don't give up on God to get you through whatever it is you are suffering now. He is the only one who can heal you, lead you to the right people who can help you, or deliver you from pain and suffering. Keep praying for Him to move powerfully on your behalf.

There are countless other common fears, such as the fear of failure; the fear of losing control; the fear of being hurt, injured, or destroyed; and the fear of not having enough, to name a few. No matter what fear you are dealing with, say in the face of it, "My God shall supply" all my needs "according to His riches in glory by Christ Jesus" (Philippians 4:19). Trust God to give you what you need when you need it.

Prayer Power

Lord, where I have allowed fears from the past to affect my life in a negative way now, I pray You would reveal that to me so I can be free of them. Help me to forget the past and move forward today with the new life You have for me. Free me from all destructive fear so I can do what You want me to do. Enable me to stand strong in You and never give in to fear or become discouraged. Teach me how to believe and speak Your Word whenever fear threatens to weaken me. Help me to rise above it.

If I am talking to people—whether just a few or many—take away all fear and give me Your strength, power, and clarity of mind. Give me Your love for each person I talk to and help me to see them through *Your* eyes. Open their spiritual eyes, ears, and heart to hear Your Spirit speaking to them.

Show me any place in my mind where a specific fear has taken hold that will keep me from the liberty You have for me. I ask that You will be fully in control of my life so that I can be a slave to Your righteousness and not a slave to fear. Teach me to live in and be motivated by Your perfect love, which casts out tormenting fear (1 John 4:18). Thank You, Lord, that You are able to deliver me from all my fears (Psalm 34:4). I ask You to do that now.

In Jesus' name I pray.

WORD POWER

There is no fear in love; but perfect love casts out fear,
because fear involves torment.
But he who fears has not been made perfect in love.

1 John 4:18

I sought the Lord, and He heard me,
and delivered me from all my fears.

Psalm 34:4

The Lord is my helper; I will not fear.
What can man do to me?

Hebrews 13:6

In You, O Lord, I put my trust;
Let me never be ashamed;
deliver me in Your righteousness.

Psalm 31:1

He delivered me because He delighted in me.

Psalm 18:19

3

What Does the Bible Say About Fear?

The Bible contains a number of stories about people overcoming their fear and doing what God told them to do. David was a perfect example because he spoke often about being afraid. Yet faced his fear head-on with faith and prayer.

David saw evil proliferating around him and said, "The *pangs of death surrounded me*, and the *floods of ungodliness made me afraid...the snares of death confronted me*. In my distress *I called upon the LORD*, and cried out to my God; *He heard my voice* from His temple, and my cry came before Him" (Psalm 18:4-6).

How many of us who love God have felt the same way when we experienced fear, for whatever reason? When fear invades your heart and mind, it's important to know what God says in order to get the right perspective. The following sections of this chapter are about what God has said in His Word to those of us who love Him. We must keep each one in mind in order to keep fear from controlling us.

God Shields You When You Seek His Protection

King David often had to flee to safety from those who were against him, including his son Absalom. Rising up in defiance against his father, Absalom led many others in his nation to do so as well. But David prayed, "Lord, how they have increased who trouble me! Many are they who rise up against me. Many are they who say of me, 'There is no help for him in God.' *But You, O Lord, are a shield for me*, my glory and the One who lifts up my head" (Psalm 3:1-3).

David knew where his help came from, and he prayed in faith because he trusted God. People were saying that even God couldn't save David. But he fervently prayed, saying, "I cried to the Lord with my voice, and He heard me from His holy hill...I lay down and slept; I awoke, for the Lord sustained me. *I will not be afraid of ten thousands of people who have set themselves against me all around*" (Psalm 3:4-6).

That is great *faith* in God.

When David prayed, he believed God heard him. So he was able to sleep at night because he knew God was his shield of protection. We need to know that as well. That takes knowing God and His Word, walking with Him in prayer, and expressing gratefulness for all His blessings—including His protection.

God Frees You from Fear and Anxiety

We all have times when we want to escape everything that makes us afraid or anxious. David—a man after God's own heart—did too. When he was betrayed by a friend, he said he wanted to "wander far off, and remain in the wilderness" (Psalm 55:7).

Haven't we all felt like that at certain times?

But David went on to tell what he had decided to do in the face of his fear-filled situation. "As for me, *I will call upon God, and the LORD shall save me. Evening and morning and at noon I will pray*, and cry aloud, and He shall hear my voice. *He has redeemed my soul in peace from the battle that was against me*, for there were many against me" (Psalm 55:16-18).

God gave David peace and comfort in place of fear and anxiety because David walked closely with Him and had faith in the one true God and in the power of His Word.

We, too, have to pray the same way—with strong faith—and believe God will redeem our anxious soul. If we become so afraid that we are overwhelmed by the horror of what we fear, we must pray unceasingly—morning, noon, and night—until we receive the peace of God in our situation. God will do that for us.

David said, "*Cast your burden on the LORD, and He shall sustain you*; He *shall never permit the righteous to be moved*" (Psalm 55:22). What a great and encouraging word this is to us. When we are faithful to seek the Lord and live His way, He is faithful to protect us.

The apostle Paul said, "*Be anxious for nothing, but in everything by prayer* and supplication, with thanksgiving, let your requests be made known to God; and the peace of God, which surpasses all understanding, will guard your hearts and minds through Christ Jesus" (Philippians 4:6-7). God is saying that to you now. Don't let yourself suffer with fear and anxiety about anything! Instead, pray and be thankful, and He will give you amazing peace.

God Enables You to See Your Situation from *His* Perspective

When the king of Syria was going to war against Israel, Elisha the prophet was advising the king of Israel on what God had revealed to Elisha about Syria. When the king of Syria found out Elisha was revealing his plans to the Israeli king, he sent an army against Elisha at night and surrounded the city where Elisha and his servant were living. When Elisha's servant got up in the morning and saw the Syrian army, he fearfully asked Elisha, "What shall we do?"

Elisha said to his servant, "'*Do not fear, for those who are with us are more than those who are with them.*' And Elisha prayed, and said, 'LORD, I pray, open his eyes that he may see.' Then the LORD opened the eyes of the young man, and he saw. And behold, the mountain was full of horses and chariots of fire all around Elisha" (2 Kings 6:16-17).

There was the army of the Lord there to protect him.

So when the Syrians came against Elisha, he prayed to the Lord, saying, "Strike this people, I pray, with blindness" (2 Kings 6:18).

God did exactly what Elisha prayed He would do.

Elisha then misled the Syrian army, saying he would lead them to himself. But instead he led them to Samaria in Israel. Then Elisha said, "'LORD, open the eyes of these men, that they may see.' And the LORD opened their eyes, and they saw; and there they were, inside Samaria!" (2 Kings 6:20).

God led the Syrians right into the land and hand of their enemy.

When the king of Israel saw that the Syrians were in his territory, he asked Elisha what to do with them, and Elisha said not to kill them, but instead to show them mercy, give them dinner, and send them home. The king of Israel did exactly that, and the Syrians never came to Israel again. (See 2 Kings 6:21-23.)

What an amazing outcome to a terribly frightening situation. It fully illustrates the mercy of God and His plans for our safety. Don't you love how Elisha could see in the spirit exactly the way God had protected him and his servant completely? Wouldn't it be amazing to see in the spirit so well that we can rest in the fact that God is with us and protecting us? Ask God to help you see things from *His* perspective. He may not show you vivid detail the way He did for Elisha and his servant, but He can give you great insight into your situation along with peace about the outcome.

God Helps You When You Fear You Can't Do It on Your Own

The Bible says to trust God to accomplish things we know we can't do on our own. A perfect example of this is when God instructed Zerubbabel—who was the governor of Judah and responsible for completing the restoration of the temple that had been torn down—that he should not trust the world's wealth or strength or human ability. This word from God to Zerubbabel at that time has now become one of the most familiar and powerful quotes in the Bible. The Lord instructed Zerubbabel as to how to build the temple saying, "*Not by might nor by power, but by My Spirit*" (Zechariah 4:6). Zerubbabel was to trust God to do it by the power of His Spirit and not to trust in the power of men.

God assured Zerubbabel that any mountain of opposition to what God had called him to do would be flattened by His grace. God said, "Who are you, O great mountain? Before Zerubbabel you shall become a plain! And *he shall bring forth the capstone with shouts of 'Grace, grace to it!'*" (Zechariah 4:7). In other words, it would be the grace of God that accomplished it.

Grace is the unmerited favor of God, meaning we did nothing to deserve it. This relates to our salvation. We are saved by grace and not by what we do. It's also by God's grace that the Holy Spirit works powerfully in us. How many times have you experienced the grace of God working through you or for you when there was no other explanation for what happened?

No matter how much discouragement you have experienced in your life, or how much resistance you have had to face while moving into the life God is calling you to live, the enemy will always come to taunt you with fearful thoughts such as, *I can't do this. I am afraid I will fail.* The enemy will accuse you of being a failure, a sinner, a mess. But you can rely on the grace of God to enable you to do what you know you cannot do on your own. You are saved by grace. You are rescued from yourself by grace. And you can shout "Grace!" to whatever situation you are facing. When you shout "Grace!" in the face of your problems, that mountain of opposition will be flattened.

God chose David's son Solomon to build the temple in Jerusalem instead of his father. David instructed Solomon saying, "*Be strong and of good courage, and do it; do not fear nor be dismayed, for the* LORD *God—my God—will be with you. He will not leave you nor forsake you,* until you have finished all the work for the service of the house of the LORD" (1 Chronicles 28:20).

Often, what God calls us to do can be daunting, and we can become afraid to even attempt it. But we can be certain that if we depend on God to *be with us,* He will also *enable* us to do what we need to do.

Greatness will not be achieved by *your* power or might. It will be *His.*

God Invites You into His Kingdom When
You Invite Him into Your Heart

Jesus said, "Unless one is born again, he cannot see the kingdom of God" (John 3:3). *He also said, "Unless one is born of water and the Spirit, he cannot enter the kingdom of God"* (John 3:5). *We cannot see or enter the kingdom of God unless we are born again.* We are born the first time in the flesh. When we are born again, it's a spiritual birth in which the transforming power of the Holy Spirit works in us. Without being born again in the spirit, we do not have a true relationship with God. Jesus said, "That which is born of the flesh is flesh, and that which is born of the Spirit is spirit" (John 3:6).

Jesus said, "I am the way, the truth, and the life. No one comes to the Father except through Me" (John 14:6). He also said, "You shall know the truth, and the truth shall make you free" (John 8:32). And it is not just *any* truth. It's knowing *His* truth. *God's* truth. That's because He *is* the truth.

Jesus said, "God so loved the world that He gave His only begotten Son, that whoever believes in Him should not perish but have everlasting life" (John 3:16). God loved us so much that He gave His Son, Jesus, to pay the price for our sins—which is death—so that we can live forever with Him, free from death and hell.

Jesus said, "Do not fear, little flock, for it is your Father's good pleasure to give you the kingdom" (Luke 12:32). God wants us to be a part of His kingdom. But how do we get to His kingdom? We receive Jesus into our heart.

When we receive Jesus, our eyes, ears, and heart are open to many things that we could not see, hear, and understand before. It is a whole new world and a whole new life. You now can live in the realm of God's kingdom because your eyes have been opened to it.

Without a revelation from God, we can't fully sense His presence, understand His Word, or recognize His kingdom. "*The natural man does not receive the things of the Spirit of God, for they are foolishness to him*; nor can he know them, because *they are spiritually discerned*" (1 Corinthians 2:14). We only have spiritual discernment when we have the Spirit of the one true God within us giving us life in the Spirit.

God gives you the way to establish a personal relationship with Him by receiving His Son, Jesus, as your Savior. When you have done that, He frees you from all the consequences of your past sins, and that puts you in right relationship with God. You can then talk to God in prayer, and He will hear and answer.

Jesus said, "Most assuredly, I say to you, he who believes in Me has everlasting life" (John 6:47). He also said, *"Whoever confesses Me before men, him the Son of Man also will confess before the angels of God.* But he who denies Me before men will be denied before the angels of God" (Luke 12:8-9). And, "As many as received Him, *to them He gave the right to become children of God,* to those who believe in His name" (John 1:12).

Jesus told His followers that after He was resurrected He was going to the Father and would send His Holy Spirit to dwell in them. Only after Jesus had given His life in order to pay the consequences for our sins and was resurrected would He be able to send the Holy Spirt to dwell in those who believed in Him. The Holy Spirit cannot dwell in an unsanctified person. Those of us who receive Jesus are sanctified by the blood of Jesus, and so the Holy Spirit can live in us.

Paul said, "You are not in the flesh but in the Spirit, if indeed the Spirit of God dwells in you. Now if anyone does not have the Spirit of Christ, he is not His" (Romans 8:9). The Spirit of Christ is the Holy Spirit of God. There is only one Holy Spirit. God the Father; Jesus Christ, His Son; and the Holy Spirit are three separate persons but one God. When we receive the Lord, He gives us His Spirit to live in us. God's Spirit enables us to pray in power, to understand God's Word, to talk about Jesus to others, to enable us to do what we cannot do on our own, and to worship God in a life-changing and dynamic way. The Holy Spirit of God who proceeds from the Father is the Spirit of truth. (See John 15:26.) He is also called the Helper.

Jesus has set us free from death and hell, and having His Spirit in us enables us to live our life in the Spirit, and not in continued disobedience to God's ways.

Every true Christian has the Spirit of Christ in him or her. If we say we don't have the Holy Spirit living in us, then we are not Christians. I am not talking about special outpourings of the Holy Spirit. I am simply talking about receiving Jesus and Him immediately giving us His Spirit to dwell in us. That is how He never leaves us or forsakes us. After Jesus was resurrected, He ascended into heaven, where He is at the right hand of God. He is coming back and will fulfill all His promises to do so. The Holy Spirit remains with us and never leaves us.

After Jesus rose from the dead, the disciples were afraid until the Holy Spirit emboldened them to go out and tell people the good news about Jesus. "The disciples were filled with joy and with the Holy Spirit" (Acts 13:52). *There is a connection between having joy and having the Holy Spirit in you.* The joy of the Lord rising in you comes from the Holy Spirit of God dwelling in you. Our God shares Himself with us. It doesn't get any better than that.

The truth is, we all need the Lord. That's because we "all have sinned and fall short of the glory of God" (Romans 3:23). He redeemed us, which means we are released, delivered, and set free from evil and the consequences of our own sin. If you have never received Jesus and want to now, simply say this prayer to the Lord:

> Lord Jesus, I believe You are the Son of God. Although it's hard to comprehend love so great, I believe You laid down Your life for me so that I can have life forever with You and a better life now. I believe You died on the cross and were resurrected from the dead to prove that everything You said is the truth. I confess my sins to You, and I repent of not living Your way. Help me to live Your way every day. Thank You for forgiving me and loving me and turning my life into a new beginning. Thank You for Your victory over death and hell so I don't have to live

in fear. Help me to become all You created me to be. In Your name, I pray.

You may have already received Jesus and know all this, but it is good to remember these words or words like them often so they are fresh in your mind and a part of your living in God's kingdom here on earth. It's the only way to dwell in peace and be free of incapacitating fear.

The best news is "*if anyone is in Christ, he is a new creation; old things have passed away; behold, all things have become new*" (2 Corinthians 5:17). We can truly leave our past behind because He makes us new. That means when God looks at us, He sees the beauty, purity, and sinlessness of Jesus in us. We need to see ourselves that way too and thank God for it.

God Assures You That All Things Are Possible When You Believe in Him

Having faith means believing in God's Word. It means reading His Word each day and letting it renew your heart. It means choosing to stand strong on the promises of God in His Word even when you are tempted to doubt. It means living as though you believe what God said in His Word is the truth.

Turning to God and His Word at the first sign of fear is one of the ways we grow in faith. "*Faith comes by hearing, and hearing by the word of God*" (Romans 10:17). We can't grow in faith unless we read or hear God's Word. God desires that we have such strong faith in Him and His truth that we no longer are controlled by fear.

Having faith means believing He will hear and answer your prayers, even though you don't see the manifestation of what you are believing for right away. "Faith is the substance of things hoped for, *the evidence of things not seen*" (Hebrews 11:1). Our faith is evidence that we have prayed for what has not yet appeared, and our hope is in the Lord, who hears us and will answer in His way and time.

Abraham believed that God would fulfill His promise to give him a son, even though he saw no physical possibility of that ever happening. He was about 100 years old, and his wife, Sarah, was about 90 and had passed the time of childbearing. Abraham still did not waver. He believed God would do what He had promised. That is, until they started doubting. Then they tried to help God in their own feeble way and ahead of God's schedule. (See Genesis, chapters 15 and 16.)

God "gives life to the dead and calls those things which do not exist as though they did" (Romans 4:17). We need to have faith in His ability to do that. Sarah's womb was dead, but God said it would become alive with a son she would bear. And that is eventually what happened.

The Bible says, "Without faith it is impossible to please Him, for *he who comes to God must believe that He is, and that He is a rewarder of those who diligently seek Him*" (Hebrews 11:6). With all my heart I believe in Him, and I know He has rewarded me—and will continue to reward me—because I seek Him every day. When difficult things happen and I see no good way out, I believe the God of the impossible will do something good that I didn't think was possible. I believe that because all things are possible with God.

Jesus's disciples, who had been with Him every day and witnessed His miracles, asked of Him, "Increase our faith" (Luke 17:5). The day when they were all together at their last supper, Jesus said, "*I have prayed for you, that your faith should not fail*" (Luke 22:32). He knew the fear and terror coming upon them and how horrific it would all be for them. We, too, must pray that *our* faith will not fail in frightening times in our life. The truth is, "We walk by faith, not by sight" (2 Corinthians 5:7). We can't keep looking at our problems and what is frightening us. We have to focus on what our powerful, almighty God can do and remember that nothing is impossible for Him. That is how we walk in faith.

There are many things to be afraid of, and having faith doesn't mean you will never feel afraid. Even the strongest in faith have times of fear. Faith is how we rise above the fear. *Faith is how we are healed.* "The prayer of faith will save the sick, and the Lord will raise him up. And if he has committed sins, he will be forgiven" (James 5:15). Fear can make us sick.

The truth is, "God has dealt to each one a measure of faith" (Romans 12:3). "*Whatever is not from faith is sin*" (Romans 14:23). Jesus said, "If you have faith as a mustard seed, you will say to this mountain, 'Move from here to there,' and it will move; and *nothing will be impossible for you*" (Matthew 17:20).

When a father sought healing for his young son, Jesus said to him, "If you can believe, *all things are possible to him who believes.*" Immediately the child's father cried out, "*Lord, I believe; help my unbelief!*" (Mark 9:24). The child was healed. We, too, can ask God for more faith.

The opposite of faith is doubt. James, the brother of Jesus, described doubt. "He who doubts is like a wave of the sea driven and tossed by the wind" (James 1:6). Jesus said, "*By grace you have been saved through faith*, and that not of yourselves; *it is the gift of God*" (Ephesians 2:8). We must get rid of doubt and live in the faith God has given us.

All things are possible for you if you believe in the God of the impossible and take Him at His Word. It is possible to be free of fear.

God Leads You by His Spirit

When we walk according to the flesh, we follow our own desires. We want what we want when we want it. But when we walk in the

Spirit, we follow the will of God and the leading of the Holy Spirit in us. He helps us live God's way and focus our mind on the things of God. "Those who live according to the flesh set their minds on the things of the flesh, but those who live according to the Spirit, the things of the Spirit" (Romans 8:5). We always have a choice about how we will live.

When we are fleshly minded, we are an enemy of God, and that is not a good thing. It brings death to us in many ways. When we are spiritually minded, we live to please God, and that brings us life. "The carnal mind is enmity against God; for it is not subject to the law of God, nor indeed can be. So then, those who are in the flesh cannot please God" (Romans 8:7-8).

Jesus said, "He who believes in Me, as the Scripture has said, *out of his heart will flow rivers of living water*" (John 7:38). The Holy Spirit is the source of the living water flowing from our heart.

When we receive Jesus, we are *given* the Spirit of God to live in us. He is God's gift to us. But being *led* by the Spirit from that time on is something we *choose* to do. "*As many as are led by the Spirit of God, these are sons of God*" (Romans 8:14). Who doesn't want to be a son or daughter of God and led by His Spirit?

The word "led" also means that we are *continually* being led. It's an ongoing process. It's more than knowing the laws and commandments of God; it's also being led to do the right thing in every situation. It's a prompting in our heart that helps us make the right choices or decisions. And if there are life-changing decisions, we can be led to seek the counsel of other strong believers in whom is the same Holy Spirit, and who walk according to the Spirit and not the flesh. They can confirm whether it is indeed the Spirit leading us or not.

God wants you to let the rivers of living water flow from your heart, so don't stop up the flow by entertaining doubt and unbelief.

God Loves You, And You are Valuable to Him

God says about you: "Fear not, for I have redeemed you; I have called you by your name; You are Mine" (Isaiah 43:1). He says, "*You did not receive the spirit of bondage again to fear*, but you received the Spirit of adoption by whom we cry out, 'Abba, Father'" (Romans 8:15). "Abba" is an endearing name for "Father." It's like saying "Daddy." It speaks of a close relationship.

When you have a strong father who never leaves you or abandons you and who is always there for you, you feel safe and loved, and that takes away your fear. And you *do* have one. He is your heavenly Father God, and it's His perfect love that takes away your fears. If you have incapacitating or disturbing fear, it's because you have not been perfected in God's love. That takes faith, knowing that the only perfect love is the love of God. Human love is failing and conditional. God's love is unfailing and unconditional. Believing that with all your heart requires spending time with Him.

God says about anyone who trusts in Him and puts their hope in Him that he shall "be like a tree planted by the waters, which spreads out its roots by the river, and *will not fear when heat comes*; but its leaf will be green, and *will not be anxious in the year of drought*, nor will cease from yielding fruit" (Jeremiah 17:8). When the heat is on in *your* life, you won't wither because you have a source of refreshment an unbeliever does not have. You don't have to be afraid when the economy tanks or your finances fail because God will still supply your needs.

Jesus said about *you* that "the very hairs of your head are all numbered. *Do not fear therefore; you are of more value than many sparrows*" (Luke 12:7). That means He values you. He sees the details of your life and what you need. He understands you. "The Lord knows those who are His" (2 Timothy 2:19). He knows your fears, but He wants to hear about them from you when you pray. Jesus said, "Do not be afraid" countless times. That's because He knew we would be.

The love of God, as seen through the acts of Jesus, is perfect. Receiving His love and His sacrifice of love is life changing. The closer you get to an intimate walk with God, the more you will become like Him, the more you are perfected, and the more your fears will fade.

Prayer Power

Lord, thank You for Your grace, which has saved me in every way I can be saved. Thank You that in Your mercy You have given me Your love to strengthen and heal me and take away my fear. Thank You for Your Word that reminds me You are *with* me and *for* me at all times. Therefore, I do not need to live in fear about who is against me. With You on my side, who can have victory over me? Help me to stand on Your Word and pray to You unceasingly.

Enable me to grow with unshakeable faith in You and to live my life according to the leading of Your Holy Spirit. Engrave Your Word on my heart so I never forget it. Help me to keep Your truth in my mind at all times so it becomes part of me. Thank You that out of my heart "flow rivers of living water" that come from Your Holy Spirit in me (John 7:38). Help me to never stop that flow by my unbelief.

I thank You for Your power to free me from the grip of fear and anxiety. Thank You that when You call me to do something that frightens me, You will be with me and enable me to do it. Protect me from the things I fear and from all dangers lurking about that I am not even aware of yet. Teach me to never forget that You are always with me. Enable me to see the things that frighten me from Your perspective. Help me to do all I need to do.

Show me how to live in Your kingdom by the power of Your Spirit and not in the world according to my own desires. Increase my faith every day as I read Your Word and walk with You. Thank You that You love me and I am valuable to You.

In Jesus' name I pray.

WORD POWER

I am the door. If anyone enters by Me, he will be saved,
and will go in and out and find pasture.

JOHN 10:9

God is our refuge and strength,
a very present help in trouble.

PSALM 46:1

Fear not, for I am with you; be not dismayed,
for I am your God.
I will strengthen you, yes, I will help you,
I will uphold you with My righteous right hand.

ISAIAH 41:10

This poor man cried out, and the LORD heard him,
and saved him out of all his troubles.

PSALM 34:6

The LORD is good, a stronghold in the day of trouble;
and He knows those who trust in Him.

NAHUM 1:7

4

What Is the Fear God
Allows Us to Experience?

Not every fear is bad. God allows us to experience some fear as part of His protection for us. This kind of fear can save our life. So it's possible for fear to be a good thing, but we must be able to discern when that is true. Any fear that hurts us, cripples and tortures us, or leads us away from a close relationship with God is a destructive fear—the kind God does not want us to have. Any fear that turns us toward God, draws us closer to Him, keeps us safe, or causes us to do the right thing is good. For example, if we allow sin to creep into our lives, we will be afraid until we take it before God and repent of it. "If you do evil, be afraid" (Romans 13:4). The Holy Spirit will convict us of what we do that does not please God.

Feeling fear can actually be a prompting of the Holy Spirit, and we should not ignore that. Instead, we must bring it to God and ask for discernment. He will tell you whether there is wisdom in heeding it or if there is no basis for your fear. If there is good reason for your fear, ask Him for immediate guidance. It could be some danger He wants you to know about and take action. Or He may be calling you to pray about something that is frightening to other people.

Dangers can be anywhere. We are wise to be aware of that and continually pray for direction. You can be minding your own business at your workplace, at a public event, in school, in your own home or car, or in a common public place, and the violent plans of evil can suddenly invade that space. That's why we need to ask God for wisdom about every decision we make, everyplace we go, and whatever we do. If we don't have peace about any of those things, we cannot act as though we do. We must not stop praying and asking until we receive clear direction.

Some people appear fearless, and they do dangerous things without checking in with God for guidance. Without God, they are foolish and not wise. This can be especially true of people who have not experienced frightening situations or do not understand the possible consequences of doing irresponsible things. For example, how many young women have put themselves in vulnerable positions without a thought that someone motivated by evil could be observing them? We hear of too many women who go out for a run alone in the countryside or park at early evening and aren't seen again until their body is found later on.

That's why having healthy fear is necessary. These women are not fearless. They are clueless. They don't think anything could happen to them. They don't understand that evil can be anywhere, and we must not set ourselves up to be the prey of evil people. When we anticipate possible danger or the presence of evil, good fear will cause us to wisely put ourselves in a better position. Good fear can save our life from many dangers. Healthy fear is a call to seek God for guidance and protection.

One of the most horrific statistics is how many women are killed by their husband or boyfriend. And equally horrifying are the number of children killed by a parent in a single year. We must be in prayer for families we know. Understanding that bad things can happen at any time will keep you in prayer every day for your own safety and the safety of your loved ones. If you ever sense that you or your children are in danger of any kind because of a spouse or boyfriend, get away from that danger immediately. Don't become a statistic because you think you are doing the noble thing by staying, or you are fearless and don't think it could happen to you.

The kind of fear God *allows* will always draw you closer to Him in prayer and deeper into His Word for strength and direction, and it helps you to gain a clearer leading of His Holy Spirit.

Don't Assume Anything; Don't Think You Know Everything

Only *God* knows everything. *We* don't. Some people think they do, but that is never a good thing. Good fear keeps us from assuming we know it all. King David prayed that God would keep him from "secret faults" and "presumptuous sins" (Psalm 19:12-13). We need that kind of godly wisdom in our heart and mind. "If anyone thinks that he knows anything, he knows nothing yet as he ought to know" (1 Corinthians 8:2).

David said, "*The law of the* LORD *is perfect*, converting the soul; the testimony of the LORD is sure, *making wise the simple*; the statutes of the LORD are right, *rejoicing the heart*; the commandment of the LORD is pure, *enlightening the eyes*" (Psalm 19:7-8). David went on to say of God's commandments that "*by them Your servant is warned*, and in keeping them there is great reward" (Psalm 19:11). The Word of God warns us and gives us godly wisdom.

The Bible exposes what is in our soul. It makes us wise and warns us of danger.

God's Word tells us His will for us. For example, we know from the Word that God's will is that we love and worship Him, obey His commandments, and love others. But we cannot assume we know His will for our life concerning all the variables that are unique to us, such as whom we marry, what house we live in, where we work, and what we do in our spare time. We must seek God and rely on Him to show us what we need to know concerning these things. That means being in close contact with Him in prayer, in His Word, and in worship every day. And to do it early, at the beginning of the day if possible. We can't leave home without the guidance, direction, and wisdom of the Holy Spirit of God in our mind and heart.

Reading God's Word, praying, worshipping God, and obeying Him is doing our part, but we also need to be *aware* of what is going on around us and *wise* to what is possible. That takes walking closely with God. For example, how many times have we heard in the news about a young woman who was raped and murdered, only to find out that she was drinking in a bar late at night and either walked home alone or drove home by herself? Rape and murder are never the victim's fault, no matter how easily the woman makes it for the perpetrator. It's always the fault of the rapist and murderer. But in some cases, even a smidgen of godly discernment, wisdom, and sense of fear of what is possible could have possibly saved the life of one of these girls.

We all need to seek wisdom and discernment about whether we should include certain people in our personal lives or not. How many women have allowed the wrong man into her life, and that turned out to be the worst decision she ever made? What didn't she see before the situation turned deadly for her? I am in no way blaming the woman because men like that are masters of deception and disguise. They put great effort into keeping their true character a secret from their prey. The reverse is also true as well. How many men have let the wrong woman into his life, and that was a disastrous mistake? He toyed with her emotions and then left her, and she retaliated.

We must not ignore any uneasy feelings or fear we have about someone or some situation, because they can be warning signs that urge us to take a different route. We need to listen to our gut feelings, which God allows us to have for our own good.

Every fear we have should lead us to God in prayer and to be in His Word for guidance.

We should ask God if our fears are legitimate concerns, or completely advanced by the lies of the enemy, or totally unfounded. God does not want fear torturing us, but He does want to give us discernment in every situation. The fear God allows will lead us to Him for protection.

We all have unfortunately learned by this time not to assume that nothing can ever go wrong at our children's schools. Long before any of the school shootings occurred, the thought that children wouldn't be safe in school didn't enter our mind. We parents were concerned mostly about how other kids could harm ours, or expose them to some form of evil, or could bully them and make them afraid. We always prayed for their safety, but we never even remotely imagined the horrific things that have happened in schools in recent years.

After I wrote *The Power of a Praying Parent*, I spent years speaking at different schools and encouraging parents to start prayer groups at their children's schools or in their own home in order to pray for their children and the safety of the school itself. Moms and grandmothers came in droves, and many of them ended up meeting one morning a week at the school or in someone's house.

These godly moms had a healthy fear of what *could* happen. They also had an understanding of the power of prayer and faith in God's Word, and what God could do in response to their prayers. They met with the intention of praying for God's covering of protection over the children and the school in every way possible. These were all Christian schools I spoke at because in many cases God and Christianity are shut out of public schools and private non-Christian schools as well. But any mom can still have a small prayer group in her own home or apartment that meets regularly.

Jesus said, "Where *two or three* are gathered together in My name, *I am there in the midst of them*" (Matthew 18:20). The promise that the presence of God will be there when we pray together, with even one other person, is not to be taken lightly. This is why I have had a prayer group in my house that meets once a week for more than 30 years. We are all afraid of what could happen if we don't pray. And that is a good fear.

The encroachment of evil has gone so far beyond our greatest fears and has brought every believing parent to their knees in prayer and dependence upon God. Because praying for our children never ends until we go to be with the Lord, I wrote *The Power of Praying for Your Adult Children*. We parents all know that our concerns for our children don't stop when they leave the house. In fact, they increase. The evil that threatens their lives never stops, so we must never stop keeping them covered in prayer, no matter what age they are. My children are in their thirties and forties, and I still keep praying for them in my prayer group. And now I pray for my grandchildren as well.

We can never assume we know everything.

Don't Ignore Your God-Given Discernment

God gives instruction, guidance, warnings, and sensitivity about people and situations. Whether we take heed of our gut feelings or not is up to us. We don't have to live in anxiety all the time, but we need discernment. There will be situations where we have to make a decision in an instant, and we must be able to trust our instincts enough to choose the right one. We can discern if what we are feeling is actually the prompting of the Holy Spirit to our heart. We should always ask God to show us if our hesitation or uneasy feeling is from Him. Keep in mind that God allows us to experience fear at times in order to turn us toward Him—our ultimate place of safety. He wants us to seek Him for guidance in everything we do or allow into our lives.

Don't push aside a suspicion you have about a person or situation. If something makes you feel unsafe, whisper a prayer immediately. Say, "Lord, be in charge of this situation. Show me what I should do and enable me to do it." If you feel intimidated or afraid of someone at any time—especially your husband or wife—do not ignore these feelings. Remove yourself from that person as quickly as possible.

Anger is a big red flag. People who are angry all the time are at greater risk for heart attacks, and they are also more likely to do harm to themselves or others. Anger has to have someplace to go—either inward or outward. If an angry person causes you to feel fearful, leave their presence. Ask God immediately what you should do. Say, "Lord, show me what to do about this angry person who makes me feel afraid." Then do what God shows you.

God wants us to seek Him about *everyone* we allow into our lives. He wants us to have a close walk with Him—seeking Him in prayer every day, praising Him often, reading His Word daily—because these things add up to being able to hear His voice to our heart and mind.

If you turn down the volume of your life every day so you can hear the quiet voice of the Lord speaking to your heart, you will be better able to trust your instincts. If you still your soul enough to listen to His instructions, He will tell you, "Don't go that way. Go *this* way." "Don't go to this place. Go there instead." He may say, "The concern you feel about this certain person is from Me, so don't go with him." "Don't walk home alone in the dark."

When you can hear the prompting of the Lord, it will save your life in every way. Don't deny your intuitive side when you walk with

God. The fear you feel may be a gift from Him so the Holy Spirit can guide you to a place of safety.

Don't Underplay Your Fear of Harassment

As I said above, we must each choose carefully the person or people we let into our life.

I learned this the hard way. I used to think, *It's always good to help someone, right? It's always good to let someone into your home you have seen at church because they must be godly.* I did that years ago without even asking God about it. I had no fear because what eventually transpired had never even entered my mind. So I wasn't praying about it until I realized what was going on. By then it was too late.

When my children were just starting a new year in grade school, a young woman was at the school waiting for me when I picked up my children to take them home. As it turned out, her son was in the same class as my son. She was kind, sweet, and friendly as she introduced herself as Sandy (not her real name). She said she'd read my autobiography and related to the details of being abused as a child. She had experienced something very similar with one of her parents, although I gathered it was not her mother, who, she informed me, had paid for her grandson to go to this little private Christian school. Plus, judging from some of the things she said, I suspected her abuse included something of a sexual nature, which I had always thought of as far more damaging to the soul of a child than any other form of abuse. I didn't ask for any details. I just listened. She thanked me for giving her hope that she could one day recover from her past. She asked where we attended church, and I told her.

Every day after school when I went to pick up my children, she was there waiting to talk to me. We talked mostly about recovering from emotional trauma. I met her mother, her son, and her husband, and they all seemed to be a very nice family.

That following Sunday morning, my family and I went to church, and I dropped off each of my children in their respective classrooms as usual. But as I entered the sanctuary, Sandy was waiting for me at the door. I was happy to see that she and her family had decided to attend church there. As it turned out, they lived in an apartment close by.

Her husband had a business that helped homeowners with the maintenance of their home, and she assisted him. So when she told me that their business was extremely slow, I hired them to do some work on my father's house. After my mother died, we had helped him move into a smaller home about an hour away from us. I saw that their work was good quality, so I asked them to do some work on our house as well.

Sandy mentioned she needed to have her hair repaired because she had tried to dye her dark hair a light shade of blond and totally fried it. She asked who and where my hair dresser was, and I told her. She also found out what stores I went to and what services I attended during the week at church. All the while I believed I was helping a person in need, not realizing I was walking into a trap.

Gradually, nearly every place I went, Sandy would be out front waiting for me. I realized how terribly needy she was, but it troubled me that she felt I had all the answers to help her rise above her emotional torment. I pointed her to the Lord in every way I could, but she insisted that I was the only one who could help her. This unhealthy dependency was a bad sign, so I told her that only the Lord and a good Christian counselor could truly help her, but I would pray for her to be healed and set free.

When I realized what was happening over the next couple months and how serious it was, I tried to steer her toward professional help. But she was focused on me fixing everything *for* her. She said she thought I could become the mother she never had, which surprised me. Apparently, her mother never came to her rescue from the abuser. I appealed to her husband to get help for her, but although he was painfully aware of her problem, he, too, hoped I could help her. He told my husband and me that he was at the end of his rope with her since she had become frightening to him and their son and her own mother as well.

The more I tried to distance myself from her, the more she tried to include herself in my life. Soon she began acting bizarrely and calling my home 30 to 40 times a day with demonic-sounding voices on my answering machine, threatening to kill my children if I didn't help her. It became apparent, and was also confirmed by her husband, that she had multiple personalities. Her behavior frightened us because we didn't know what she was capable of doing.

Often, in the middle of the night, she would come to our house, climb over the fence into our backyard, and look into our windows. She told me she did this and proved it by describing something in the house that only someone who had been there would have seen. My husband, Michael, and I prayed continually for God to remove this terrifying burden from us. And we asked other close friends to pray with us as well. But nothing changed.

We called the police, and the policeman who came to our house informed us that they could not do anything "until the stalker has broken in."

"It's too late then," I pleaded. "Something has to be done *before that!*"

They advised us to get a lawyer and seek a restraining order against her. We did, and surprisingly she appeared in court. The judge sternly warned her to stop stalking me and my family, but that didn't slow her down at all. The phone calls and threats kept coming, as if the restraining order never even happened. I feared for our lives every moment. We called the police a number of times, but we were always told that they could do nothing unless the person had broken into the house and threatened our lives from the inside.

Our experience then was that a restraining order is useless in keeping a crazy person away from you. The order means nothing to the stalker. But you must have one because when you do call the police to report that person for breaking in, they know who it is. And the good news is that if you do get killed, the suspicion is on the person named in the restraining order. I am sure you agree, however, this news is not good enough.

When I asked the policeman what else he advised that we do, he said, "You could either hire bodyguards or move somewhere else." Neither of those options appealed to us because of the major expense of it all. But we ended up doing both. The policeman gave me the name of a security company to call, and we hired two bodyguards to protect our home for ten hours at night so we could sleep. They were so expensive that we knew this form of protection was completely unsustainable, but we felt we had no other choice at that moment. The possibilities of an insane stalker following through on specific threats couldn't be minimized or ignored.

The bodyguards reported to us a number of times that they saw the stalker coming up the street to our house, sometimes driving and sometimes walking. Each time, once she saw them she left immediately.

I could tell by her many threatening phone calls each day that she was getting worse. She had turned from a sweet young woman to someone who acted as if she was demon possessed. My fear was unbearable, and it was affecting my health because I was unable to get enough sleep. We kept all this from our children, not wanting to frighten them. And I watched closely over them.

Next, we chose the only option we had left and sold our house. The sale went through quickly, which I believe was God's answer to our prayers. We moved quietly and secretly to another town and left no forwarding address. I stopped going to all the places I formerly did and found new places instead.

It was the most frightening time in my life as a believer. I knew there was no way out of this situation unless God did a miracle. We prayed He would act on our behalf and save us from the enemy, who was working through Sandy to torment us with fear. We prayed God would take her out of our lives to someplace where she could find help. He eventually answered that prayer.

I found out later from someone who knew her family that her husband and mother were able to have her committed to a mental hospital in a town several hours south of us. After that, we entered into a time of much-needed peace. But I never forgot how horrible the fear is when your life and the lives of your children are threatened and there appears to be no way out. We felt powerless. I also saw how God protected us because we prayed fervently about our fears, and He opened up a way to safety that only He could do.

I realized how naive I was back then. My assumptions were wrong. I assumed that because a person goes to church and puts their children in a Christian school, that means they are good, trustworthy, or safe. I was so wrong. We have to ask God to show us the truth about all people and whom we can trust with our personal life. How many people would attest to that if only they were alive today to do so?

Jesus knew the heart, character, and intentions of every person He met while He was on earth. He still knows the heart, character, and intentions of every person, and by His Spirit He will reveal that to us when we ask Him to do so. But we have to ask Him for that kind of discernment and not wait until we are in a crisis.

A person doesn't have to be a stalker in order to be a harasser. Anyone who is obsessed with another person and is unnerving to be around is out of line. That abnormality can be seriously amped up when the object of that person's obsession wants to put an end to it.

Know that someone being nice to you does not mean he or she is a good or sane person. Don't believe that other people are just like you and think like you and are as decent as you. Because you are a kind and thoughtful person doesn't mean every other person is as well.

If ever you are suspicious of someone or some situation, pay attention to that. If you feel hesitant to get on an elevator with one man in it—or even a woman—don't do it. Turn around and walk the other way as if you just remembered something you need to do. This protective fear is God given, so thank Him for every warning or awareness you have. Don't ever minimize your fear of being harassed by someone.

Ask God for discernment that only He can give you. Don't admonish yourself if you feel afraid. Ask Him to show you the truth about a person or situation and how to follow your common sense instincts. Ask Him to reveal the fear He allows for your safety and protection.

Take seriously every anxious and fearful feeling you have and bring them to God. Stay close to Him so you always hear His voice speaking to your heart. Pray before you go anywhere and before you make any decision about where you go and what you do. Thank Him in advance for His warnings and promptings.

Don't Neglect to Surrender to What
God Is Telling You to Do

God sometimes asks us to surrender to the very thing we fear, dread, or don't want to do. That's because He wants us to die to what we cling to and turn to Him. But we must know clearly it's God's will, and that we understand God's Word to our heart.

Jeremiah the prophet proclaimed to Zedekiah, the king of Judah, a word from God, saying, "*If you surely surrender* to the king of Babylon's princes, then your soul shall live; this city shall not be burned with fire, and you and your house shall live. *But if you do not surrender* to the king of Babylon's princes, then this city shall be given into the hand of the Chaldeans; they shall burn it with fire, and you shall not escape from their hand" (Jeremiah 38:17-18).

This is not what Zedekiah wanted to hear. In fact, it was the exact opposite of what he was thinking. God was saying if the king surrendered to this enemy, he would be saved from the other enemy. When the king said he was afraid to do that, Jeremiah said, "Please, *obey the voice of the LORD which I speak to you. So it shall be well with you, and your soul shall live*" (Jeremiah 38:20).

Instead of praying to be right with God, the king continued to rebel against Him, so all that God had warned him about came upon him and his people. He should have surrendered his life to God and obeyed what God told him to do.

Daniel, a mighty man of God, reminded his people that disaster would come upon them, as it was written in the law of Moses, if they didn't come before God and repent of their sins. (See Deuteronomy 28:15-20.) Even when Daniel informed his people that the disaster they feared had come upon them because they had not obeyed God, they still refused to give up their sin. (See Daniel 9:13-14.)

Daniel confessed to God the sins of the people and prayed that God's anger would be turned away and He would spare Jerusalem. Daniel prayed, "We have sinned, we have done wickedly! O Lord, according to all Your righteousness, I pray, let Your anger and Your fury be turned away from Your city Jerusalem" (Daniel 9:15-16). Even though Daniel's own life was impeccably righteous, and he was a powerful intercessor, he appealed to God's mercy on behalf of the sinful people.

Daniel asked God to hear his prayer—not because he or the people were good, but because God is a merciful God. Daniel prayed, "O my God, incline Your ear and hear...for we do not present our supplications before You because of our righteous deeds, but *because of Your great mercies*" (Daniel 9:18).

Daniel fasted and prayed for three full weeks because of the terrible state of Jerusalem. (See Daniel 10:2-3.) Finally, an angelic being appeared to Daniel and caused him to tremble with fear. The angel said, "*Do not fear, Daniel, for from the first day that you set your heart to understand, and to humble yourself before your God, your words were heard;* and I have come because of your words. *But the prince of the kingdom of Persia withstood me twenty-one days;* and behold, Michael, one of the chief princes, came to help me, for I had been left alone there with the kings of Persia" (Daniel 10:12-13). Daniel's prayers were heard, but there was a spiritual battle going on that delayed God's answer.

Not only does this illustrate clearly how prayer and fasting can affect the outcome of situations on earth, but even when we don't yet see answers to our prayers, we can trust that God is still working on our behalf when we are surrendered to Him.

Jesus said, "He who is of God hears God's words" (John 8:47). *When we are surrendered to God, we hear Him when He speaks to our heart.* Jesus also said that He could do nothing by Himself. (See John 5:30.) He, too, needed the power of God.

Just like Jesus, we need the power of God working in us so we can do what He wants us to do. God will empower those of us who are committed to Him to resist the fear that comes upon us and enable us to rise above it.

God allows us to experience certain fear because in the process He teaches us to trust Him. We can trust that our "tribulation produces *perseverance*; and perseverance, *character*; and character, *hope*" (Romans 5:3-4). And all this happens "*because the love of God has been poured out in our hearts by the Holy Spirit who was given to us*" (Romans 5:5).

When we glorify God during a period of tribulation by praising and exalting Him, we learn how to *persevere*, grow in *character*, and live in *hope.* The reason we have hope is because the love of God has been poured into us by the Holy Spirit, who lives in our heart.

Don't Fail to Produce the Fruit of the Spirit

When we walk with God by the power of His Spirit in us every day, the fruit of the Spirit grows in us. (See Galatians 5:22-23.) These virtues are not something we can produce by our own efforts. They appear in us when we are Spirit controlled. If we stop producing the fruit, we have reason to be afraid. That's because we are not living the way God wants us to live. When we don't live God's way, we don't have peace. We have fear, unrest, anxiety, and dread instead. When we don't depend on God and His Word, we don't know how to live His way, nor do we have the strength and power of God enabling us to do it. Having the fruit of the Spirit in us is a sign that we are on the right path. The fruit of the Spirit are God's qualities that He gives us when we surrender our lives to Him and allow Him to work in us. And they are given to us at a depth we cannot possibly attain on our own.

There are nine fruit of the Spirit in the Bible.

The first three fruit of the Spirit in us are love, joy, and peace.

These fruit can only come from God in their fullest dimension. That's because only He is all of these things. He *is* love. He *is* joy. He *is* peace. He pours Himself into us by the power of His Spirit in us. Without Him, we cannot begin to produce love, joy, and peace to the degree He wants for us. We are given love so complete and unconditional that it heals and sustains us. We can extend our own shallow love, be peaceful for a few moments, and try to conjure up what we think is joy, but those things are fleeting, if at all.

These fruit can only come from God in their fullest dimension. That's because only He is all of these things. He is love. He is joy. He is peace. He pours Himself into us by the power of His Spirit in us. Without Him, we cannot begin to produce love, joy, and peace to the degree He wants for us. We are given love so complete and unconditional that it heals and sustains us. We can extend our own shallow love, be peaceful for a few moments, and try to conjure up what we think is joy, but those things are fleeting. These virtues are not momentary; they are unfailing. That's because they come from God, and *He* is unfailing. His love is unfailing and unconditional. The peace *He* gives us doesn't waver. The joy we feel is like a magnificent and lasting sunrise in our heart such as we have never even imagined. These fruit cannot be experienced outside of our connection to Him and His Spirit in us.

The next three fruit of the Spirit are patience, kindness, and goodness.

They have to do with our attitude and actions toward others. If we are consistently patient, kind, and good to other people, we are exhibiting the characteristics of God. That doesn't mean we decide to be patient in a particular moment, or we choose to be kind to a particular person for a few minutes a day, or that we are good when people are watching. It means we are patient, kind, and good to others all day, everyday, because that is who we are. We don't pick and choose our patient moments. We don't decide to be nice now that the other person is doing what we want. We don't determine to do something good today to make up for all the times we didn't.

When we are truly led by the Spirit, and the seeds of the fruit of the Spirit are planted in us by the Holy Spirit, we produce an abundant crop because that is who we have become. That doesn't mean we never lapse. A lapse means we allowed our flesh to temporarily make some decision and have power in our lives. It means we are not walking in the Spirit. But we can swiftly rectify that by confessing and repenting of our lapse and again drawing close to God.

The last three of the nine fruit of the Spirit are faithfulness, gentleness, and *self-control.*

These fruit have to do with the way we should live and our godly character. When we are guided by being faithful and gentle, and having self-control, we will do the right thing. If we find ourself misbehaving or developing an attitude that is opposed to these fruit of the Spirit, it should set off alarms in our mind and heart that we are not walking in the Spirit of God.

If you find yourself being mean, nasty, rude, harsh, disrespecting of, and out of control in front of others, or are directing that sin toward someone, go before the Lord immediately and confess it to Him. Be willing to give up what you think is your right to be that way. Then confess what you have done to the people in front of whom you expressed it. Realize that in being nasty, mean, or rude, you have hurt yourself far more than you have hurt others. You have grieved the Spirit of God and will not be able to experience the fullness of His presence working in you until you make it right.

You need to also realize this same thing about others who hurt *you*. If they are mean, rude, nasty, harsh, out of control, and disrespecting toward you, keep in mind that these people are hurting themselves more than they are hurting you. They will experience the consequences for it—or lack of blessings—just as you would if you chose to behave that way.

A person who is faithful keeps promises; is loyal, reliable, dependable, trustworthy, and steadfast; maintains an unchanging allegiance to God; and does what is good in God's eyes. A faithless person does none of the above.

A person who has gentleness as a characteristic is caring of others, sensitive to their needs, and not given to panic. A person who does not have gentleness as a characteristic is bombastic, shocking, insensitive to others, and one who happily rushes to blurt out bad news or words that could hurt someone.

A person who has self-control is always able to do the right thing at the right time. They don't give in to their flesh and spill words that will upset or destroy someone. People without self-control are avoided by most people, except for people who are as out of control as they are.

The fruit of the Spirit is produced in us as we walk in the Spirit of God. If we are not producing these fruits in our life, then we are not living a Spirit-led life. "If we live in the Spirit, let us also walk in the Spirit" (Galatians 5:25). It is as simple as that. We determine how we will walk. Jesus said of believers, "You will know them by their fruits" (Matthew 7:16). When you are led by the Holy Spirit, the fruit of the Spirt is manifested in you. It won't be you in your own strength trying to make it happen. It will happen because it is not in you to do otherwise.

Too many believers rely on their own efforts and not God's power. They are drawn to the world instead of God. Too many people, especially young people, are falling away from certain churches and denominations because they do not see the love and power of God. Those churches insist on defining God by what they perceive His limitations to be and refuse to acknowledge the work and power of His Holy Spirit. There has never been a time when people didn't need the power of God in their lives and the love He has for them. That need is increasing daily, not decreasing.

When the church offers no answers and does not manifest the love, peace, joy, and the rest of the fruit of the Spirit in the believers, then it ceases to be relevant. If people don't sense God's presence and power, they think it isn't real and they don't want it. We are the church. The church Jesus is coming back for is not a bunch of buildings. It is His people who believe in Him and in whom the Holy Spirit dwells, and in whom He sees are producing good fruit.

Fear can be a good thing or a bad thing. Good fear calls you to pray. Bad fear takes over your life and controls you. Good fear is a response to danger that inspires you to take steps to protect yourself and others, and to alleviate the danger in some way. Good fear leads you closer to God. When God directs your path, you will end up in the right place at the right time, so you have nothing to fear. The evidence of God's favor is the fruit of His Spirit manifested in you.

Prayer Power

Lord, help me to clearly discern the promptings of Your Spirit to my heart and mind so that I never foolishly ignore them. Teach me to pray whenever I have fear or a sense of danger or intuition about persons or situations that are not good. Keep me and my family and friends away from dangerous places and always aware of the possible plans of evil people. Give us discernment and warnings when we are not where we are supposed to be.

Help me to trust in You with all my heart and not depend on my own understanding. Help me to acknowledge You in everything I do and depend on You to direct me wherever I go. Keep me "from presumptuous sins; let them not have dominion over me...then I shall be blameless, and I shall be innocent of great transgression" (Psalm 19:13). Keep me from assuming anything by neglecting to take everything to You. I don't ever want to think I know everything about a person, place, or situation. I want to hear the truth from You.

Help me to choose every day to walk with the leading of Your Holy Spirit and not be led by my flesh. Produce in me the fruit of Your Spirit. Fill me with Your love, peace, and joy so that I will be more like You. Make me patient, kind, and good to others. Cause me to be faithful and gentle and always exhibiting great self-control. Teach me to pray unceasingly about everything so I can always be at the right place at the right time.

In Jesus' name I pray.

WORD POWER

Every good tree bears good fruit,
but a bad tree bears bad fruit.

MATTHEW 7:17

By this My Father is glorified, that you bear much fruit;
so you will be My disciples.

JOHN 15:8

You did not choose Me,
but I chose you and appointed you
that you should go and bear fruit,
and that your fruit should remain,
that whatever you ask the Father in My name
He may give you.

JOHN 15:16

I am the true vine, and My Father is the vinedresser.
Every branch in Me that does not bear fruit He takes away;
and every branch that bears fruit He prunes,
that it may bear more fruit.

JOHN 15:1-2

The fruit of the Spirit is love, joy, peace,
longsuffering, kindness, goodness, faithfulness,
gentleness, self-control.

GALATIANS 5:22-23

5

What Is the Fear God Wants Us to Have?

Countless words have been written about fear in the Bible. For the most part, it's divided between the fear God *does not want us* to entertain and the fear God *wants us to have*. The only fear God wants us to have is a fear of *Him*. That doesn't mean we live in terror that God will strike us with lightning if He is mad at us. The fear of God the Bible talks about is actually such a deep reverence for Him that it makes us afraid of what our life would be like without Him.

God wants us to love Him so much and know Him so well that we will not fear doing His will, but rather we will fear *not* doing His will. And we do this not because we fear God is looking for ways to destroy us, but because we want to please Him and not miss out on everything He has for us—most of all, the fullness of His presence.

God called Moses to go to Egypt, which was dangerous because he was wanted there for murdering an Egyptian. But God told Moses to fear *Him* and *not men*. Even though the Angel of the Lord appeared to Moses in a burning bush that was not being consumed by the fire, and even though God spoke to Moses about wanting to deliver His people from slavery in Egypt, and even though God did miraculous things in front of Moses to convince him of the miracles He would do, Moses still protested, saying he was not an eloquent enough speaker to go before Pharaoh with God's message. The Lord was not pleased with that, but He allowed Aaron, Moses' brother, to be the speaker instead. So God would tell Moses what to say, and Moses would tell Aaron, and Aaron would tell Pharaoh. Moses would still be the one God chose to do this, even though Moses did not believe God could do such a great miracle as to make him a speaker anyone would listen to. (See Exodus chapters 3 and 4 for full details of this amazing story.)

Having the fear of God makes us wise enough to know we must do what God is calling us to do, because we will be miserable if we don't. The fear of God causes us to seek God's guidance, because we fear the consequences of going off on our own and not pleasing Him.

Moses told the people of Israel, after God brought them out of slavery, that what the Lord required of them was *"to fear the LORD your God*, to *walk in all His ways* and to *love Him*, to *serve the LORD your God* with *all your heart* and with *all your soul"* (Deuteronomy 10:12). That word is for us too. It's what He requires of each of us today. We need to remember at all times to *fear God, live His way, love Him unfailingly, and serve Him wholeheartedly.*

The fear of God is more than just obeying His commandments, although that is a big part of it. It is a full heart of love and awe-filled respect for the Lord. "These people draw near with their mouths and honor Me with their lips, but *have removed their hearts far from Me*, and their fear toward Me is taught by the commandment of men" (Isaiah 29:13). The fear of the Lord is felt in the heart. When we have the fear of God in our heart, we don't want to disappoint or grieve Him in any way.

Jesus said, "I will show you whom you should fear: *Fear Him who, after He has killed, has power to cast into hell*; yes, I say to you, fear Him!" (Luke 12:5). God has power over who spends eternity with Him and who does not. He is the One with whom you want to have your most important relationship.

The Benefits of Having the Fear of God

Countless blessings and benefits come from fearing God—which means having a devoted and loving heart toward Him. Below are some of them.

1. *When we have the fear of God, He guides us into His will.* "Who is the man that fears the LORD? Him shall He teach in the way He chooses" (Psalm 25:12). We do not ever want to be out of the will of God. *That* is frightening.

2. *When we have the fear of God, we are afraid to not obey His commandments and laws.* "My flesh trembles for fear of You, and I am afraid of Your judgments" (Psalm 119:120). We know how serious it is to not obey God because His laws are there for our own good.

3. *When we have the fear of God, He hears our prayers and gives us the desires of our heart.* "He will fulfill the desire of those who fear Him; He also will hear their cry and save them" (Psalm 145:19). People who don't have the fear of God in their heart think praying is telling God what to do. And if He doesn't do what they want, they turn on Him. But praying is how we communicate with God. It is one of the ways we show our love for Him.

4. *When we have the fear of God, we are given assurance concerning His blessings on our children.* "In the fear of the LORD there is strong confidence, and His children will have a place of refuge" (Proverbs

14:26). When we have the fear of the Lord, He not only blesses us, but confidence in God produces the opposite of fear. He blesses our children as well.

5. *When we have the fear of God, we are able to separate ourselves from evil.* "By the fear of the LORD one departs from evil" (Proverbs 16:6). When we don't have the fear of God, we can get sucked into the enemy's plan for our life and away from God's plan. When we have the fear of God, we have discernment to see when we need to walk away from evil.

6. *When we have the fear of God, we are given special knowledge.* "The secret of the LORD is with those who fear Him, and He will show them His covenant" (Psalm 25:14). This secret knowledge will be revealed to us when we need it. There will be protection, provision, and blessings beyond what we would have had otherwise. (See Psalm 25:12-15.)

7. *When we have the fear of God, we experience the goodness of God.* "Oh, how great is Your goodness, which You have laid up for those who fear You, which You have prepared for those who trust in You" (Psalm 31:19). That means we will have blessings ahead that we don't even know about yet because God has already prepared them for us.

8. *When we have the fear of God, we please Him.* "The LORD takes pleasure in those who fear Him, in those who hope in His mercy" (Psalm 147:11). Our desire toward God is to walk with Him and to please Him. He is pleased by our reverence, love, and devotion to Him

9. *When we have the fear of God, He shares Himself with us.* "His divine power has given to us all things that pertain to life and godliness, through the knowledge of Him who called us by glory and

virtue, by which have been given to us exceedingly great and precious promises, that *through these you may be partakers of the divine nature*, having escaped the corruption that is in the world through lust" (2 Peter 1:3-4). This is the most amazing thing. God wants us to be partakers of His divine nature. That means God will impart who He is to us. He shares His love, peace, power, and so much more with those who reverence Him. The more time we spend with Him in His Word, talking to Him in prayer, and worshipping Him, the more He pours Himself into us and the more we become like Him.

10. *When we have the fear of God, we live His way and enjoy a full life.* The Bible says we are to "fear the LORD your God, to keep all His statutes and His commandments which I command you, you and your son and your grandson, all the days of your life, and that your days may be prolonged" (Deuteronomy 6:2). The fear of God protects us from what could shorten our life. And not only us, but also it affects our children and grandchildren. It would be wise for us to pray that our children and grandchildren—or nieces and nephews if you do not have children—will have the fear of the Lord.

The Truth About God-Fearing People

1. *People who fear God are watched over.* "The eye of the LORD is on those who fear Him, on those who hope in His mercy" (Psalm 33:18). We look to Him with reverence in our heart, and He watches over us. The knowledge of that can take away our fear.

2. *People who fear God find deliverance.* "The angel of the LORD encamps all around those who fear Him, and delivers them" (Psalm 34:7). I love this promise. I have recalled it many times when I've been in a vulnerable position and I knew someone evil could easily have taken advantage of that. Yet I was kept safe.

3. *People who fear God find mercy.* "As the heavens are high above the earth, so great is His mercy toward those who fear Him" (Psalm 103:11). We all need the mercy of God extended to us because we cannot make it through life without it. His mercy is great toward us, and it is unfailing—just as *He* is.

4. *People who fear God find life works better for them.* "Oh, that they had such a heart in them that they would fear Me and always keep all My commandments, that it might be well with them and with their children forever!" (Deuteronomy 5:29). Our fear of God and obedience to Him bring many blessings on us and our children, and that is what God longs to give us.

5. *People who fear God receive His compassion.* "As a father pities his children, so the LORD pities those who fear Him" (Psalm 103:13). The Lord has a compassionate heart toward those who reverence Him. That is what mercy is all about.

6. *People who fear God receive mercy, and so do their offspring.* "The mercy of the LORD is from everlasting to everlasting on those who fear Him, and His righteousness to children's children" (Psalm 103:17). God blesses not only our children but our grandchildren as well. What a great reward for a life well lived in reverence and love for God.

7. *People who fear God are helped and protected.* "You who fear the LORD, trust in the LORD; He is their help and their shield" (Psalm 115:11). You will find that God will help and protect you beyond what you can even think to pray about when you deeply and unfailingly reverence Him.

8. *People who fear God enjoy a full life.* "The fear of the LORD prolongs days, but the years of the wicked will be shortened" (Proverbs 10:27). God watches over those who fear Him.

9. *People who fear God are blessed.* "He will bless those who fear the LORD, both small and great" (Psalm 115:13). He pours out blessings upon us because we have the fear of God in our heart. It will be beyond what we think about, and it will surprise us.

10. *People who fear God find healing.* "To you who fear My name the Sun of Righteousness shall arise with healing in His wings" (Malachi 4:2). God heals those who love and reverence Him.

11. *People who fear God hate what He hates.* "The fear of the LORD is to hate evil; pride and arrogance and the evil way and the perverse mouth I hate" (Proverbs 8:13). We can see those things in our society, and we hate them as much as God does.

12. *People who fear God find contentment in life.* "The fear of the LORD leads to life, and he who has it will abide in satisfaction; he will not be visited with evil" (Proverbs 19:23). People who fear God are more content than those who don't. And we are kept from evil. All that brings strength and healing to us.

13. *People who fear God are not prideful, and so they are rewarded.* "By humility and the fear of the LORD are riches and honor and life" (Proverbs 22:4). When we reverence God, we don't become arrogant. We are focused on God and not ourselves.

14. *People who fear God are not burdened with jealousy.* "Do not let your heart envy sinners, but be zealous for the fear of the LORD all the day" (Proverbs 23:17). Jealousy and the fear of the Lord do not live in the same vessel.

15. *People who fear God bless others around them.* "Those who fear You will be glad when they see me, because I have hoped in Your word" (Psalm 119:74). I love that verse. It always reminds me of the wife of

one of my pastors, who was an inspiration to me her whole life. Just seeing someone so strong in faith and hope gave me strength and hope. Those who love God passionately and revere Him faithfully give us strength when we see them. Their strong faith and hope in the Lord strengthens our faith and hope too. We all feel good and secure when we are around people who reverence God, believe in His Word, and live His way.

The many men and women of the Bible who did great things for God all had one thing in common—they had the fear of the Lord. They loved God and reverenced Him and did what He asked of them no matter how much it frightened them or how hard it was for them. Without the fear of God in their heart, Noah would not have built the ark, Moses would not have confronted Pharaoh, Esther would not have saved her people from death, Nehemiah would have never built the wall, and the disciples would have never carried the good news about the redemptive accomplishments of Jesus on the cross to the rest of the world. The fear of God in us allows God to do great things through us.

The Benefits of Having Godly Wisdom

Having great reverence for God gives us a steady flow of wisdom that leads us away from people and situations that could destroy us. "The fear of the LORD is a fountain of life, to turn one away from the snares of death" (Proverbs 14:27).

Jesus is referred to in the Bible as "Christ the *power* of God and the *wisdom* of God" (1 Corinthians 1:24). It says that Christ Jesus "became for us wisdom from God—and *righteousness* and *sanctification* and *redemption*" (1 Corinthians 1:30). It's only by receiving Jesus and having His Holy Spirit in us that we have full access to the wisdom of God. We cannot have godly wisdom apart from God's

Spirit of wisdom in us. The Bible says that in God the Father and Christ the Son are hidden "all the treasures of wisdom and knowledge" (Colossians 2:3).

The wisdom and knowledge God gives us will stabilize and strengthen us even in shaky times and uncertain situations. "*Wisdom and knowledge* will be the stability of your times, and the *strength* of salvation; the *fear of the* LORD is His treasure" (Isaiah 33:6). *The fear of the Lord is a treasure He gives us.* And we treasure Him for that.

The Bible says, "If any of you lacks wisdom, let him ask of God, who gives to all liberally and without reproach, and it will be given to him" (James 1:5). It says about wisdom, "If you cry out for discernment, and lift up your voice for understanding...*then you will understand the fear of the* LORD, *and find the knowledge of God. For the* LORD *gives wisdom*" (Proverbs 2:3,5-6).

The fear of the Lord is total reliance on God. When we pray for wisdom, He gives it to us.

God gives us wisdom when we seek His knowledge and understanding instead of relying on our own. "The fear of the LORD is the beginning of wisdom, and the knowledge of the Holy One is understanding" (Proverbs 9:10). When we have godly wisdom, we are led to do the right things in situations where, if left to ourselves, we wouldn't know what to do.

It says of God that "*He stores up sound wisdom for the upright*; He is a shield to those who walk uprightly; He guards the paths of justice, and *preserves the way of His saints*...When wisdom enters your heart, and knowledge is pleasant to your soul, *discretion will preserve you*; understanding will keep you, *to deliver you from the way of evil*" (Proverbs 2:7-12). Wisdom protects us from evil and makes our way safe.

Having wisdom can keep you from being ruled by fear. "Keep sound wisdom and discretion; so *they will be life to your soul* and grace to your neck. Then you *will walk safely* in your way, and *your foot will not stumble*. When you lie down, *you will not be afraid*; yes, you will lie down and your sleep will be sweet" (Proverbs 3:21-24). We all need that and thank God for it.

The Truth About Godly Wisdom
Versus Worldly Wisdom

There is a huge difference between God-fearing people and godless people who don't have the fear of God in their heart. David wrote, "Concerning the transgression of the wicked: There is no fear of God before his eyes" (Psalm 36:1). The reason our society has become so corrupt is because people do not fear God. Their god is money, power, control, influence, and more. They think they will not have to answer for their evil because they believe there is no God.

True wisdom is actually the wisdom of God that He gives us. The wisdom of this world is nothing by comparison. If we only listen to the "wisdom" coming from the world, we will never understand the truth. Worldly wisdom is always foolish. God's truth always wins in the end. "Let no one deceive himself. If anyone among you seems to be wise in this age, let him become a fool that he may become wise. For *the wisdom of this world is foolishness with God*. For it is written, 'He catches the wise in their own craftiness'" (1 Corinthians 3:18-19). That is talking about the "worldly wise."

All the scheming, shrewd, unscrupulously clever actions of people who do not have the fear of God will trap them in their own worldly wisdom. "*The* LORD *knows the thoughts of the wise, that they are futile*" (1 Corinthians 3:20). If we don't have *the fear of God*, then we don't have godly wisdom. Worldly wisdom leads people to make foolish mistakes.

*Having wisdom from God—that comes with the fear of the Lord—
leads us away from a spirit of fear, which is not from God, but rather
from the world.*

God's wisdom is often the opposite of what the world says is wise.
The cross is the perfect example of that. The world saw Jesus' death
as a complete failure when actually it was His greatest victory and
accomplishment. "The message of the cross is foolishness to those
who are perishing, but to us who are being saved *it is the power of
God*" (1 Corinthians 1:18). The message of the cross seems foolish to
those who are not born into the kingdom of God. But it is the absolute power of God to those of us who have received Jesus and now
have the Holy Spirit. The wisdom of the world is foolish, and those
who have godly wisdom can see that.

"The foolishness of God is wiser than men, and the weakness of
God is stronger than men" (1 Corinthians 1:25). So what the world
saw as weakness in Jesus going to the cross is actually the power of
God giving us victory over sin, hell, and death. The wisdom of God
is a mystery to those whose spirit has not been reborn and ignited
by the Holy Spirit of God. And it says of the rulers of that age that,
"had they known, they would *not* have crucified the Lord of glory"
(1 Corinthians 2:8). Only God knows everything.

Having the power of God means that as you humble yourself
before God, seek Him in your life, and declare that you love and
reverence Him and never want to live a day without Him, then He
will prove to be to you all He *proclaims* to be in His Word.

The apostle Paul wrote that he did not speak with the "wisdom
of this age, nor of the rulers of this age, who are coming to nothing"
(1 Corinthians 2:6). But rather *he spoke with the wisdom of God that is
hidden from certain people* until God reveals it to others, according to
His will. That's why those who served evil did not understand what

God's plan was for the crucifixion of Jesus and the redemption of the world. They couldn't see it because they lived for their flesh and to serve the evil enemies of God. Only to the believers who feared God did He reveal His plan. He will reveal things to you that you need to see, and it will make all the difference in your life. The wisdom and understanding He gives you will be powerful because you have the fear of God in your heart.

Prayer Power

Lord, I want to be the "companion of all who fear You, and of those who keep Your precepts" (Psalm 119:63). "Teach me Your way, O LORD; I will walk in Your truth; unite my heart to Your name" (Psalm 86:11). Enable me to be filled with the knowledge of Your will. Give me the wisdom, discernment, and spiritual understanding to walk in ways that are pleasing to You.

Teach me to treasure Your commands and laws in my heart at all times. Help me to acknowledge You in everything I do so You can direct my paths. Enable me to live in Your presence, because every time I sense Your presence, it takes away all my fear. Help me to be a true God-fearing person. Give me godly wisdom so that I don't fall for the wisdom of this world. Give me the knowledge and understanding I need to live according to Your plan and purpose. Keep me from ever being wise in my own eyes, but rather help me to fear You and stay away from evil.

Thank You that You give "strength and power" to Your people (Psalm 68:35). Thank You that "You have given me the heritage of those who fear Your name" (Psalm 61:5). My reverence and love for You is great because Your presence in my life is my greatest treasure.

In Jesus' name I pray.

WORD POWER

Let all the earth fear the LORD;
let all the inhabitants of the world stand in awe of Him.

PSALM 33:8

Come, you children, listen to me;
I will teach you the fear of the LORD.

PSALM 34:11

Do not be wise in your own eyes;
fear the LORD and depart from evil.

PROVERBS 3:7

Oh, fear the LORD, you His saints!
There is no want to those who fear Him.
The young lions lack and suffer hunger;
but those who seek the LORD shall not lack any good thing.

PSALM 34:9-10

The fear of the LORD is the beginning of knowledge,
but fools despise wisdom and instruction.

PROVERBS 1:7

6

What Must We Think, Say, and Pray When We Are Afraid?

Whenever I write a book, it's as if the enemy of my soul is saying, *You think you know how to pray for your children? What are you going to do with this?* Or, *You think you know how to keep your marriage together? See if you can handle this problem.* As a result, I have learned how to rise above all that and stand on the truth of God's Word. I have learned how to pray through it. And I also know how to pray with other people when I am troubled by what is happening.

So I was not surprised when I was inundated with fear while writing this book. My fears came about partly because of all the horrifying things that were happening in the world around me, which I saw every night on the news. And I feared all these things could happen to my family, friends, neighbors, or in my town or country. The other part of what I believe God was allowing me to feel temporarily is what many people feel nearly every day of their lives.

I wasn't dealing with irrational, controlling fear. Yet my experience was still tormenting, and my sleep was not as peaceful as it had been. I knew if I was experiencing fear like this, surely countless other people were experiencing the same thing—or even worse.

I thought, *If I am in such a battle against fear, how intense must it be for others who don't know the power of God to set us free and the great impact God's Word can have on our lives? Even those of us who do know all that still need a reminder—a place we can go to in our mind, heart, soul, and spirit that immediately brings us to the truth of God.*

As I explained earlier, I had been liberated from the incapacitating fears I experienced before I became a believer. After I received the Lord and established an ever-deepening walk with Him, I was set free from a *spirit of fear* that had tormented me for decades. So I knew what I recently experienced when writing this book was that God was requiring me to listen strictly to Him and not the world. He wanted me to think the right thoughts, say the right words, and pray in a powerful way every time fear threatened to destroy my peace. And it worked. I believe He wants me to share that with you.

What we think affects who we are and who we become. It determines how we react to people and situations. Anyone can be afraid for whatever reason—but what our thoughts are when confronted with fear will influence our reaction to it.

What we all need is an immediate fast track to the peace God has for us. Then we can combat fear before it can build into something worse. If we have certain passages from God's truth to think about and proclaim in the face of our fears, plus a strong yet simple prayer to pray immediately, it would strengthen us and calm our fears. This would prevent a spirit of fear from trying to torment us.

The rest of this chapter gives you truths to guide you to a place of safety and comfort that God has for you whenever you feel afraid.

They can powerfully help you beat back the spirit of fear the enemy wants you to buy into so that you will be weakened and neutralized. God never wants you to be harassed by fear. He wants you to stand on His Word and believe what He says instead. The last section of this chapter is a tool for you to use the moment you sense fear of any kind creeping into your heart and mind. If you do these "Twenty Things to *Think, Say,* and *Pray* When You Are Afraid" enough times, they will become a habit in your mind and heart that you can summon instantly.

The Bible teaches that "the effective fervent prayer of a righteous man avails much" (James 5:16). The definition of "fervent" is to be full of zeal. God wants us to think about the truth, speak His Word boldly, and pray powerfully. Doing that changes things.

Consider the Value of Constant and Consistent Prayer

Jesus has overcome the world and all that is in it. But His people must pray. And too many of them are not doing that. They *think* about praying. They *talk* about praying. They *read* about praying. And they *think* about *talking* about *reading* about praying. But they don't pray. I know this because I have heard about it from countless people countless times for decades. That has been one of the most shocking realizations for me as a believer.

I know you have a heart for God and are a person of prayer, or you would not be reading this book. But many people don't have that mind-set, and they need to be encouraged. Once I became a believer in Jesus, some kind of miraculous breakthrough always happened for me every time I prayed, or was prayed for, or when I prayed with someone. (When you pray for someone else, *you* get blessed too.) Since I have walked with God, I have never taken the great privilege of talking to God in prayer lightly or casually.

When Peter was put in prison for his faith, believers were praying ongoingly for him. "Peter was therefore kept in prison, but *constant prayer* was offered to God for him by the church" (Acts 12:5). What happened as a result of those prayers was *"an angel of the Lord stood by him*, and a light shone in the prison; and he struck Peter on the side and raised him up, saying, 'Arise quickly!' And his *chains fell off his hands"* (Acts 12:7). Then the angel said, "Put on your garment and follow me" (Acts 12:8). After they went past the first and the second guard posts, the iron gate that led to the city opened by itself. When they went out, the angel left him (Acts 12:10). Peter knew that God had sent His angel to deliver him from prison, which was a miracle in response to unceasing prayers of the believers who had been praying. (See Acts 12:9-11.)

Never underestimate the power of your prayers that can break your chains and set you free—free from all your fears.

Consider the Value of Worshipping God

When Paul and Silas were beaten and put in prison, they weren't complaining. They *"were praying and singing hymns to God*, and the prisoners were listening to them. Suddenly there was a great earthquake, so that the foundations of the prison were shaken; and *immediately all the doors were opened and everyone's chains were loosed"* (Acts 16:25-26).

When the prison keeper woke up and saw that the prison doors were open, he assumed that the prisoners had left. He knew he would be tortured and killed for allowing that, so he "drew his sword and was about to kill himself" (Acts 16:27).

That's when Paul said loudly, "Do yourself no harm, for we are all here" (Acts 16:28). The prison keeper trembled and fell down saying, "What must I do to be saved?" (Acts 16:30). They answered, *"Believe on the Lord Jesus Christ, and you will be saved, you and your household"* (Acts 16:31). The prison keeper saw that miracle and received Jesus.

You are set free in more ways than you may know every time you worship God. *You* can be set free of fear every time you worship God as well.

Consider the Value of the Holy Spirit Helping You to Pray

The Bible says, "The Spirit also helps in our weaknesses. For we do not know what we should pray for as we ought, *but the Spirit Himself makes intercession for us* with groanings which cannot be uttered" and "*He makes intercession for the saints according to the will of God*" (Romans 8:26-27).

The Holy Spirit doesn't pray *instead* of us. He *helps* us to pray. He partners with us and makes our weak prayers strong. When we pray fervently, sometimes we don't have the words to express the depth of what we are feeling. The Holy Spirit helps us with that. God knows what the mind of the Spirit is because He intercedes for us according to God's will.

The next verse says, "*And we know that all things work together for good to those who love God*, to those who are the called according to His purpose" (Romans 8:28). That sentence is connected to the verse before it with the word "And." Can it be that there is a connection between things working out for good and us praying? Do they work out better when we allow the Holy Spirit to help us pray? I say, "How could they not?" We've all seen many times in our lives, and the lives of others, the things that don't automatically work out for good when we don't pray. Not praying is not an option if we want things to work out for good.

Consider the Value of Renewing Your Mind Every Day

It's good to offer yourself to God every day—to serve Him and do His will. Say, "I present myself and my life to You, Lord. Use me to do Your will." Paul said, "I beseech you therefore, brethren, by the mercies of God, that you *present your bodies a living sacrifice, holy, acceptable to God,* which is your reasonable service" (Romans 12:1).

Right after that he said, *"And do not be conformed to this world, but be transformed by the renewing of your mind, that you may prove what is that good and acceptable and perfect will of God"* (Romans 12:2). We are bombarded by the world system that has access to us in many ways, but we are not to *conform* to it because it is godless and full of self-obsession and idol worship. Godless people are blinded to the truth of who God really is. We are to live in the world but not be a part of the godless world mind.

We who love God must let Him renew our mind every day so that we are freshly committed to the ways of the Lord and sensitive to the beauty of His presence. We do that by worshipping God and praising Him for all He has done for us. We do it by talking to Him in prayer and reading His Word. And we have to cleanse our mind of all that is not of Him and soak in His refreshing and purifying stream until we are renewed and transformed. When we do that, we prove that God's will for our lives is not only acceptable and good, but it's also perfect.

God does not want us to think of ourselves more highly than we should. But that doesn't mean we should think of ourselves as worth nothing. Jesus considered us worth dying for, so let's not contradict Him.

Consider the Value of Confessing Your Belief in Jesus

Salvation comes to you not only because you believe in your heart Jesus is Lord, but also because you confess it with your mouth to the Lord and to the people God puts in your life. Our words of faith in Jesus seal the deal from our side. The work of salvation from God's side was sealed by all Jesus accomplished on the cross. What we do from our side is to not keep it a secret.

We go from salvation through faith to walking out our salvation every day so that we grow in faith from there. We choose to believe that God will provide everything we need for our life, including protection, provision, deliverance, and guidance. We choose to not only believe in God's promises to us in His Word, but we must also *declare His promises out loud to ourselves* daily. That way the words of our lips speak the truth to our mind and our heart, and to anyone who asks about the hope within us. The reality of Jesus in our heart has to become part of us and not something we debate with ourselves over and over when our faith is tested. And believe me, it will be. During those times, we need to be certain of God's truth.

Jesus told His disciples He was preparing them for His departure. This must have terrified them. But Jesus said He would leave His peace with them and enable them to go wherever He sent them to testify as to who He is and what He has accomplished. (See John 13:31–14:14.)

Jesus has left His peace with us as well and wants us to testify to what we know about who He is and what He has done. His peace cannot be found in the world. We must seek the peace of God at all times by being immersed in His Word and in His presence, and by praising Him and declaring who He is with our mouth.

Twenty Things to *Think, Say,* and *Pray* When You Are Afraid

1. Think about this: *God is always with me. He never leaves nor forsakes me.*

    Say boldly: "He Himself has said, 'I will never leave you nor forsake you.' So we may boldly say: 'The LORD is my helper; I will not fear. What can man do to me?'" (Hebrews 13:5-6).

    Pray powerfully: Thank You, Lord, that You will never leave me nor forsake me. Thank You that You are with me now, and I don't have to fear danger or lack.

2. Think about this: *God is always on my side.*

    Say boldly: "The LORD is on my side; I will not fear. What can man do to me?" (Psalm 118:6).

    Pray powerfully: Thank You, Lord, that You are always on my side, so I don't have to be afraid of what evil people try to do to me. You are for me, so who can succeed against me?

3. Think about this: *God is my place of safety, so I will not be afraid.*

    Say boldly: "God is our refuge and strength, a very present help in trouble. Therefore we will not fear, even though the earth be removed, and though the mountains be carried into the midst of the sea" (Psalm 46:1-2).

    Pray powerfully: Lord, You are my refuge and my help in times of trouble. Thank You for giving me Your comfort and strength so I don't have to be afraid.

4. Think about this: *God has not given me a spirit of fear.*

    Say boldly: "God has not given us a spirit of fear, but of power and of love and of a sound mind" (2 Timothy 1:7).

Pray powerfully: Thank You, Lord, that a spirit of fear never comes from You. Thank You for Your love and Your power, and for the sound mind You have given me. I receive all that from You now as I confess my fear and ask You to take it from me.

5. Think about this: *God is more powerful than anything I fear.*
   Say boldly: "Be strong in the Lord and in the power of His might" (Ephesians 6:10).
   Pray powerfully: Lord, no one is greater than You. You are more powerful than anything I face. Destroy everything that threatens me. Make me strong in You.

6. Think about this: *My help is in the name of the Lord.*
   Say boldly: "Our help is in the name of the LORD, who made heaven and earth" (Psalm 124:8).
   Pray powerfully: Jesus, Jesus, Jesus. Your name is far above every other. Thank You that my help is in Your name.

7. Think about this: *God is my strength, and I don't have to be afraid.*
   Say boldly: "The LORD is my light and my salvation; whom shall I fear? The LORD is the strength of my life; of whom shall I be afraid?" (Psalm 27:1).
   Pray powerfully: Lord, You are my strength, and Your power takes away my fear. No one is more powerful than You.

8. Think about this: *I don't have to be afraid of sudden terror.*
   Say boldly: "Do not be afraid of sudden terror, nor of trouble from the wicked when it comes; for the LORD will be your confidence, and will keep your foot from being caught" (Proverbs 3:25-26).

Pray powerfully: Lord, thank You that I don't have to fear sudden terror or trouble from wicked people because my confidence is in You. Protect me always from the works of evil.

9. Think about this: *God protects me from evil.*

    Say boldly: "'No weapon formed against you shall prosper, and every tongue which rises against you in judgment You shall condemn. This is the heritage of the servants of the LORD, and their righteousness is from Me,' says the Lord" (Isaiah 54:17).

    Pray powerfully: Lord, thank You that no weapon formed against me will prosper. And You will protect me from all who speak against me.

10. Think about this: *When I worship God, it conquers every fear.*

    Say boldly: "Enter into His gates with thanksgiving, and into His courts with praise. Be thankful to Him, and bless His name. For the LORD is good; His mercy is everlasting, and His truth endures to all generations" (Psalm 100:4-5).

    Pray powerfully: Lord, I enter Your presence with gratefulness and praise. I worship You and thank You for Your goodness and mercy toward me, and for Your unfailing Word.

11. Think about this: *God has angels watching out for me.*

    Say boldly: "He shall give His angels charge over you, to keep you in all your ways" (Psalm 91:11).

    Pray powerfully: Surround me with Your angels, Lord, and give them charge over me to keep me safe in every way.

12. Think about this: *God is for me, so who can triumph over me?*

    Say boldly: "If God is for us, who can be against us?" (Romans 8:31).

Pray powerfully: Lord, thank You that because You are for me, no one can succeed against me.

13. Think about this: *Jesus strengthens me to do what I need to do.*
    Say boldly: "I can do all things through Christ who strengthens me" (Philippians 4:13).
    Pray powerfully: Thank You, God, that I can do all the things I need to do because You strengthen me and enable me to do them.

14. Think about this: *Jesus has given me the Holy Spirit to be my Helper.*
    Say boldly: "I will pray the Father, and He will give you another Helper, that He may abide with you forever—the Spirit of truth, whom the world cannot receive, because it neither sees Him nor knows Him; but you know Him, for He dwells with you and will be in you" (John 14:16-17).
    Pray powerfully: Lord Jesus, thank You that You have given me the Holy Spirit to live in me as my Helper and Comforter—Your Spirit of truth—forever. With such great power in me, I refuse to live in fear.

15. Think about this: *God's perfect love in me takes away my fear.*
    Say boldly: "There is no fear in love; but perfect love casts out fear, because fear involves torment. But he who fears has not been made perfect in love" (1 John 4:18).
    Pray powerfully: Lord, thank You that You love me with unfailing and unconditional love. Perfect Your love in me so that I am never tormented by fear. Fill me with Your love to the point of overflowing.

16. Think about this: *God can do more than I ask or think by the power of His Spirit in me.*

    Say boldly: "To Him who is able to do exceedingly abundantly above all that we ask or think, according to the power that works in us, to Him be glory" (Ephesians 3:20-21).

    Pray powerfully: Lord, thank You that You can do more in me and my life than I can ever think of to ask. I pray that Your power working in and through me will bring down every stronghold of fear.

17. Think about this: *I follow Jesus, and therefore I will not walk in darkness.*

    Say boldly: "Jesus said, 'I am the light of the world. He who follows Me shall not walk in darkness, but have the light of life'" (John 8:12).

    Pray powerfully: Lord, thank You that because You are the light of the world and the light of my life, and I follow You, I can refuse to be pulled into the darkness of fear and doubt.

18. Think about this: *I can go to Jesus whenever I need more of Him.*

    Say boldly: "Jesus said, 'If anyone thirsts, let him come to Me and drink. He who believes in Me, as the Scripture has said, out of his heart will flow rivers of living water'" (John 7:37-38).

    Pray powerfully: Lord, thank You that because I have received You and Your Spirit in me, out of my heart will flow rivers of living water. Flow through me now and wash away all fear. Fill me with Your love, peace, and joy and bring a flow of healing to my mind, spirit, heart, and body.

19. Think about this: *God answers my prayers when I pray in Jesus' name.*

   Say boldly: "Whatever you ask in My name, that I will do, that the Father may be glorified in the Son. If you ask anything in My name, I will do it" (John 14:13-14).

   Pray powerfully: Lord, thank You that You hear my prayers and will answer me. I ask in Jesus' name that You release me from any grip of fear I feel, and free me from whatever threatens me.

20. Think about this: *Jesus gives me His incomprehensible peace.*

   Say boldly: "My peace I give to you; not as the world gives do I give to you. Let not your heart be troubled, neither let it be afraid" (John 14:27).

   Pray powerfully: Lord, thank You that I don't need to be troubled or afraid because You have given me Your peace that is far beyond anything I can even comprehend. Pour out Your peace upon me now and take away all my fear.

Prayer Power

Lord, help me to remember everything I need to recall from Your Word, especially whenever I am afraid. Enable me to speak Your Word boldly in the face of the things that frighten me. Even if there is no one else around, I will declare what I believe because Your Word gives me strength and peace and builds my faith. Thank You that You have "come as a light into the world," so that whoever believes in You "should not abide in darkness" (John 12:46). I don't have to live in the darkness of fear because I now live in the warmth and protection of Your healing and restoring light. Thank You that You have "overcome the world" (John 16:33).

Help me to always watch what I say, for I know that "out of the abundance of the heart the mouth speaks" (Matthew 12:34). Fill my heart with Your love and truth. Enable me to declare Your truth out loud and share it with others. Teach me to, "Pray without ceasing" (1 Thessalonians 5:17).

Thank You that I don't have to "be afraid of the terror by night, nor of the arrow that flies by day" (Psalm 91:5). Thank You that "You have also given me the shield of Your salvation; Your right hand has held me up, Your gentleness has made me great" (Psalm 18:35). "Whenever I am afraid, I will trust in You" (Psalm 56:3).

In Jesus' name I pray.

WORD POWER

In the world you will have tribulation;
but be of good cheer,
I have overcome the world.

JOHN 16:33

Be anxious for nothing,
but in everything by prayer and supplication,
with thanksgiving, let your requests be made known to God;
and the peace of God, which surpasses all understanding,
will guard your hearts and minds through Christ Jesus.

PHILIPPIANS 4:6-7

I have come as a light into the world,
that whoever believes in Me should not abide in darkness.

JOHN 12:46

God be merciful to us and bless us,
and cause His face to shine upon us.

PSALM 67:1

Let the words of my mouth and
the meditation of my heart
be acceptable in Your sight, O LORD,
my strength and my Redeemer.

PSALM 19:14

7

What Should We Do When We Feel Fearful?

The time I remember being most afraid in my life was when I was in my twenties.

I was living alone in a first floor apartment in a two-story apartment building in Los Angeles. I clearly recall the absolute terror I felt when I suddenly woke up in the middle of the night to the violent shaking and roar of the most terrifying earthquake I had ever been in. I'd survived a number of earthquakes before, but never like this. It was sudden, loud, and violent. The power immediately went out, and it was totally black.

I didn't know how long it would go on or how much damage it would do in the building I was living in, but I knew I could be killed. Years before, I had witnessed the aftermath of a terrible earthquake and saw the horrible results of a second floor falling in on the first floor of an apartment building. I don't think anyone was ever found alive on the bottom floor. Believe me, that memory was clearly in my mind during this earthquake.

At this time I was not a believer, so I screamed out to a god I did not know, wondering how he would hear me when I couldn't even hear myself over the deafening roar of the moving and shaking ground below and the violent rocking of the building. I could hear the sound of my dishes crashing to the floor, and my furniture and lamps hitting the walls, so I wondered how long it would be before the apartment above me would collapse on top of mine. I didn't see how it could not. I experienced such absolute terror that I decided if I lived through this, I would not live alone anymore. The thought of dying tragically all by myself was more than I could bear. I suspected that life after death could be terrifying too. I had been deep enough into the occult to know there was a spirit world, and it was frightening. I was searching for a loving god who could save me, but I'd certainly never found one there.

As I tried to make it down the short hallway from my bedroom to the living room, where my phone was, I was thrown back and forth, hitting the walls on each side of the hall so hard I was afraid I would break my shoulders. I wanted to call for help, but that was impossible. I didn't know where my phone was at that point, and I couldn't see to pick up anything, even if I were able to walk into the room. I knew I couldn't run outside because my front door was half glass, and the front of my apartment was all windows. So I had to wait in the doorframe of the hallway leading to the living room and hang on until the shaking stopped and there was no longer a danger of flying glass. When the earthquake ended, I quickly grabbed my purse and car keys and a change of clothes and got out of there and into my car before the aftershocks started. I drove to a friend's house away from all that and made plans to move.

I'd lived a life of fear before that, but this was the worst fright I'd ever experienced. The anxiety I already had began to increase from that moment on. After that, I made a lot of stupid decisions based totally on my fear. And it wasn't until I came to know the Lord several years later and experienced the full extent of His life-transforming peace that I got rid of the spirit of fear. I learned there were things I needed to do *before* anything terrifying happened, and to keep doing them until they became a way of life.

I realized it is important to monitor what we allow into our mind, and to watch what we say and pray. But there are also things we must *do* to make sure we are in the center of God's will and spending time in His presence the way He wants us to.

Because we believers have His Holy Spirit in us, He enables and empowers us to *do* what we need to *do* to live *His* way. That means not being led by our flesh, but rather being led by God's Spirit. This means continually putting to death our fleshly cravings for sinful things and choosing God's best for our life. When we do that, we have a greater sense of God's love and power, and that always takes away our fear. His love for us is unconditional. He proved that on the cross and with His resurrection. And His love is still always there for us. But if we walk outside of God's will and do our own thing, we put up a barrier between us and God, and we can't sense His presence in our lives.

We are saved by grace, but that doesn't mean God never requires us to do anything for Him. He requires us to *do many things*.

There is a problem when people think they *can do*—or *not do*—whatever they want and God's grace will cover them. It doesn't work that way. God wants us to *do* things *His* way. And He requires some action on *our* part.

The more we obey God's commands and live His way, the more we will become like Him and experience all He has for us. This includes being prompted by the Holy Spirit to *do* certain things and taking heed of what the Spirit is speaking to our heart about the specifics of our life. For example, if you are contemplating a major move or change, seek godly counselors and ask God for guidance before making this decision on your own out of fear. "Where there is no counsel, the people fall; but in the multitude of counselors there is safety" (Proverbs 11:14). We must have the mind of Christ on any decision we make. Keep in mind that God's timing is not ours.

Below are 20 things you can do when you feel afraid. Keep in mind you don't have to do all these things at once. Just take a few steps at a time according to how you feel led by the Holy Spirit.

1. Bring Every Thought into Captivity

Our thoughts can be a major burden when we have too much on our mind. If we also have any kind of fear, that makes it worse. Think about every thought you have that is troubling to you. Ask God to show you how you can replace that thought with His truth.

Say boldly: "The weapons of our warfare are not carnal but mighty in God for pulling down strongholds, casting down arguments and every high thing that exalts itself against the knowledge of God, *bringing every thought into captivity* to the obedience of Christ" (2 Corinthians 10:4-5).

Pray powerfully: Lord, I bring every negative and upsetting thought I have to You so it can be held captive in obedience to Your ways. Enable me to pull down any strongholds of fear that have been erected in my mind. I submit my mind to Your Lordship, and I refuse to allow any thoughts to weaken me with fear.

2. Commit Everything You Do to the Lord

Committing everything you do to God gives you great peace, knowing He is in charge of your life and you are waiting for His leading at all times. That calms your mind and keeps you from thinking that something terrible is going to creep up behind your back and you won't see it coming.

Say boldly: "Commit your works to the LORD, and your thoughts will be established" (Proverbs 16:3).

Pray powerfully: Lord, I commit everything I do to You for Your glory. I ask You to be in charge of my life. Establish my thoughts in clarity and calmness, and help me to never leave You out of any decision I make.

3. Decide to Trust God and Not Your Fear

God knows more than we do. He has been around longer than we have. Actually, He has always been and He knows everything. It is safe to trust His all-knowingness instead of our limited knowledge.

Say boldly: "Oh, taste and see that the LORD is good; blessed is the man who trusts in Him!" (Psalm 34:8).

Pray powerfully: Lord, I vow to trust You with all my heart and not listen to the voice of my fear. I bring every fear I have to You. Show me steps I can take to prove my trust in Your goodness toward me, and help me to take them.

4. Express Your Love for God with Praise and Worship

One way to understand the power of praise and worship is to consider the fate of those who do not praise God. The Bible says, "Since the creation of the world His invisible attributes are clearly seen, being understood by the things that are made, even His eternal power and Godhead, so that they are without excuse, because, *although they knew God, they did not glorify Him as God, nor were thankful, but became futile in their thoughts, and their foolish hearts were darkened*" (Romans 1:20-21).

Foolish and futile thoughts are depressing. Reject them by deliberately worshipping God. Every time we praise Him, there is an earthquake in the spirit realm that causes the chains that bind us to fall off and the door to our personal prison to be opened. That's because He inhabits our praise. "You are holy, enthroned in the praises of Israel" (Psalm 22:3).

Say boldly: "I will bless the LORD at all times; His praise shall continually be in my mouth. My soul shall make its boast in the LORD; the humble shall hear of it and be glad. Oh, magnify the LORD with me, and let us exalt His name together. I sought the LORD, and He heard me, and *delivered me from all my fears*" (Psalm 34:1-4).

Pray powerfully: Lord, I worship You for who You are—the almighty God of the universe and Creator of all things. I praise You for all You have done in this world and all You have done for me. Thank You that Your presence is with me every time I worship You.

5. Deliberately Focus Your Mind on Good Things

God always knows what we are thinking. That's because He looks on our heart. "The LORD knows the thoughts of man, that they are futile" (Psalm 94:11). So we must align our thinking with God, who says, "My thoughts are not your thoughts, nor are your ways My ways" (Isaiah 55:8).

Say boldly: "Whatever things are *true*, whatever things are *noble*, whatever things are *just*, whatever things are *pure*, whatever things are *lovely*, whatever things are of *good report*, if there is any *virtue* and if there is *anything praiseworthy*—meditate on these things" (Philippians 4:8).

Pray powerfully: Lord, help me to focus my mind on You and Your Word. Teach me to think about things that are true, honest, just, pure, lovely, good news, virtuous, and worthy of praise. Teach me how to fill my mind with these things.

6. Ask God if You Need to Confess Anything to Him

The Bible makes it clear that if we pretend we have no sin, and therefore nothing to confess, then we will not be prosperous in life.

"He who covers his sins will not prosper, but whoever confesses and forsakes them will have mercy" (Proverbs 28:13). Freedom from guilt doesn't just mean being free of feeling guilty. It means being free from the consequences of what we've done that has made us guilty. And these consequences happen whether we recognize our guilt or not. We must confess and repent of whatever it is God shows us. He waits to answer our prayers until we clear the slate with Him.

Say boldly: "If we say that we have no sin, we deceive ourselves, and the truth is not in us" (1 John 1:8).

Pray powerfully: Lord, show me if I have done anything that has not pleased You or is in violation of Your laws and commandments. I want to confess it to You as sin and be free of all guilt, condemnation, and the consequences of unconfessed sin. I know that if my heart does not condemn me, I have confidence toward You (1 John 3:21).

7. Be a Doer of the Word

The Bible says that it is "not the hearers of the law" who are considered good in God's eyes, but "the doers of the law will be justified" (Romans 2:13). It's not enough to just read the Word. We have to *do* what it says. When you read the Bible, ask God what He wants you to do in response to what You have read.

Say boldly: "Be doers of the word, and not hearers only, deceiving yourselves. For if anyone is a hearer of the word and not a doer, he is like a man observing his natural face in a mirror; for he observes himself, goes away, and immediately forgets what kind of man he was. But he who looks into the perfect law of liberty and continues in it, and is not a forgetful hearer but a doer of the work, this one will be blessed in what he does" (James 1:22-25).

Pray powerfully: Lord, help me to take steps each day to not only read or hear Your Word, but to actually do it. Show me what I have read or heard in Your Word that I am not doing. Enable me to take the steps I need to take.

8. Thank God for What He Has Done for You

Jesus said of the men He had healed that only one came back to thank Him. (See Luke 17:11-19.) We want to be a person who is grateful for all God has done and is doing for us daily. Be specific. Say, "Thank You for my work." "Thank You for healing me." "Thank You for what You have given me." Know that everything good in your life comes from God. (See James 1:17.)

Say boldly: "Rejoice always, pray without ceasing, in everything give thanks; for this is the will of God in Christ Jesus for you" (1 Thessalonians 5:16-18).

Pray powerfully: Lord, I thank You for everything You have given me and done for me. Thank You for the way You provide and care for me.

9. Read God's Word Daily Until
You Feel Relief from Fear

God will always speak to you through His Word. The more His Word becomes part of you, the closer your walk with Him will be. He says, "Fear not, for I am with you; be not dismayed, for I am your God. I will strengthen you, yes, I will help you, I will uphold you with My righteous right hand" (Isaiah 41:10).

Say boldly: "If you abide in Me, and My words abide in you, you will ask what you desire, and it shall be done for you" (John 15:7).

Pray powerfully: Lord, help me to set aside time to read Your Word every day and not just randomly. Teach me to read through a book of the Bible in a week or a month. Or help me to read through the Bible from beginning to end. Enable me to grow deeper in Your Word every time I read it.

10. Show Your Love for God by Living His Way

Even though David committed terrible sins—murder, adultery, and lies, to name a few—he repented of his errors and humbled himself before God. He learned hard lessons from his mistakes, but he remained a man after God's own heart.

Say boldly: "He who has My commandments and keeps them, it is he who loves Me. And he who loves Me will be loved by My Father, and I will love him and manifest Myself to him" (John 14:21).

Pray powerfully: Lord, help me to be as humble, teachable, and repentant as David was. Enable me to be a person after Your own heart. Help me to live in Your love by keeping Your commandments, so that my joy will be full. (See John 15:11.) Show me any place in my life where I am not living Your way. I know when I allow sin to stay in my life without repentance, it separates me from You.

11. Refuse to Do Anything That Will Compromise Your Walk with God

Deliberately remove anything from your life that doesn't reflect God's purity, holiness, beauty, and light. Get rid of everything that exalts other gods. *Ask* God to show you any person, activity, or situation in your life that should not be there for whatever reason. The Bible says, "You should no longer walk as the rest of the Gentiles walk, in the futility of their mind" (Ephesians 4:17). Ask Him to reveal any temptation to do something that is not His best for you. If God shows you anything like that, ask Him to give you the clarity, strength, and courage to say no to it. If you are doing something that doesn't glorify God or is destroying you, say goodbye to that idol and tell God you want to serve and glorify only Him.

Say boldly: "Watch and pray, lest you enter into temptation. The spirit indeed is willing, but the flesh is weak" (Matthew 26:41).

Pray powerfully: Lord, reveal any place in me or my life where my commitment to You is compromised. Help me to "enter by the narrow gate; for wide is the gate and broad is the way that leads to destruction, and there are many who go in by it" (Matthew 7:13). You have said to cleanse our hands and purify our heart, otherwise we are "double-minded" (James 4:8). "Search me, O God, and know my heart; try me, and know my anxieties; and see if there is any wicked way in me, and lead me in the way everlasting" (Psalm 139:23-24). Keep me from ever having one foot in Your kingdom and the other in the world, for I know You never bless that.

12. Pray and Don't Give Up

At the first sign of fear, run to the Lord in prayer. Tell Him what is in your heart, and pray He will protect you. Don't let others make you afraid that you can never be in a safe place. God can either lead you to a safer place, or He can make safe the place where you *are*. He can also hide you from evil.

Prayer is the way we communicate with God. We don't have a relationship with Him if we are not praying. One of the parables Jesus spoke was to teach us "that men always ought to pray and not lose heart" (Luke 18:1). That means we don't *give* up and stop praying. Give God time to do what His will is to do.

Say boldly: "Continue earnestly in prayer, being vigilant in it with thanksgiving" (Colossians 4:2).

Pray powerfully: Lord, help me not to become discouraged when I don't see the answers to my prayers as quickly as I would like. Enable me to continue praying no matter what happens. (See Acts 6:4.) I draw near to You now, knowing You will draw near to me (James 4:8). I am thankful for the privilege of being able to pray to You, trusting You will hear and answer.

13. Pray the Prayer Jesus Taught His Disciples

The disciples noticed that when Jesus went apart from them to pray, He came back empowered to do miracles. They made that connection between power and prayer. They didn't ask Him how to get the power. They asked Him to teach them how to pray. And Jesus taught them to pray what we now call "The Lord's Prayer."

In that prayer, Jesus taught us to acknowledge God as our *heavenly Father*—which establishes our personal relationship with Him as His children. We are to enter His holy presence in worship and praise. We are to pray for His will to be done and His kingdom to be established on earth the way it is in heaven—which means we pray that it be established in ourselves, in the people we love and care about, and in the world we live in.

He also taught us to pray that all our needs will be met by God, and that He would forgive our sins in the same way we forgive others who sin against us. This puts a convicting light on any lack of forgiveness we may harbor in our heart. We are also to ask God for the strength to withstand every temptation and be *delivered from the evil one.* Lastly, we are to declare that His kingdom and glory are forever. Jesus' name was not used in this prayer because He had not yet been crucified on the cross and resurrected.

If you are in a situation where you need to pray and don't know where to start, pray this prayer. It covers everything, and you can fill in details afterward. We can too often neglect to pray *this prayer, but we will be the poorer for it if we do.*

Say boldly: "When you pray, go into your room, and when you have shut your door, pray to your Father who is in the secret place; and your Father who sees in secret will reward you openly...For your Father knows the things you have need of before you ask Him" (Matthew 6:6,8).

Pray powerfully: "Our Father in heaven, hallowed be Your name. Your kingdom come. Your will be done on earth as it is in heaven. Give us this day our daily bread. And forgive us our debts, as we forgive our debtors. And do not lead us into temptation, but deliver us from the evil one. For Yours is the kingdom and the power and the glory forever. Amen" (Matthew 6:9-13).

14. Ask God to Help You Show Love to Others

No one has seen God, but when we show love to others, that act reveals the love of God to them. "No one has seen God at any time. If we love one another, God abides in us, and His love has been perfected in us" (1 John 4:12). People who don't love others don't know God. "He who does not love does not know God, for God is love" (1 John 4:8).

Jesus commanded us to love others. Sometimes that can be difficult without His help. If that is the case with you, ask Him to fill your heart with His love and teach you to see who needs a special act of kindness each day. It may be someone you don't know, such as a stranger whom God reveals to you as needing an expression of love, but it can also be a friend or family member. Often we don't see the true hurt or need of a person close to us. When a lawyer asked Jesus what the great commandment is, He told him to love God and love others. (See Matthew 22:34-40.) Nothing we do is more important than those two things.

Ask God to show you how to love others the way He does. This could be something as simple and life changing as simply talking to a person or praying for them. God will show you. And the reward for doing so is greater peace in your mind and soul. Sometimes praying for another person to be free of fear is a good way to help conquer your own fear.

Say boldly: "'You shall love the LORD your God with all your heart, with all your soul, and with all your mind.' This is the first and great commandment. And the second is like it: 'You shall love your neighbor as yourself'" (Matthew 22:39).

Pray powerfully: Lord, help me to show deliberate acts of love to someone today who especially needs to be affirmed, encouraged, or helped in any way. Enable me to obey Your two greatest commandments—to love You and love others. Help me to do for others what I would want them to do for me (Matthew 7:12).

15. Celebrate the Lord's Supper in Remembrance of Him

The Lord's Supper, also called Communion, is something Jesus commanded, and we need to do what He says. The purpose of it is to remind us of what He accomplished for us on the cross. It's also to receive the healing and renewal that is found in celebrating His amazing sacrifice. You may already be joining with your church to celebrate the Lord's Supper on a regular basis, but if not, you can do this alone or with one or more other people, just as Jesus commanded. Celebrate the Lord's Supper whenever you sense fear trying to overtake you. The enemy hates it when you remind him of his defeat by celebrating Jesus' victory on the cross.

Say boldly: "The Lord Jesus on the same night in which He was betrayed took bread; and when He had given thanks, He broke it and said, 'Take, eat; this is My body which is broken for you; do this in remembrance of Me.' In the same manner He also took the cup after supper, saying, 'This cup is the new covenant in My blood. This do, as often as you drink it, in remembrance of Me.' For as often as you eat this bread and drink this cup, you proclaim the Lord's death till He comes" (1 Corinthians 11:23-26).

Pray powerfully: Lord, thank You for all You accomplished on the cross. Help me never neglect to obey Your command to celebrate Communion in remembrance of You. Thank You for the healing and freedom that comes in doing so.

16. Ask God to Reveal His Will for Your Life

We don't know certain things until we ask. God's will for our life is one of them. We may *think* we know, so we don't ask God, "What is Your will for me in this situation?" Or we don't ask often enough. And when we find out what God wants, we must be quick to say, "I want what You want, Lord."

When the angel appeared to Mary to tell her that she had been chosen to give birth to the Messiah, her response was, "Let it be to me according to your word" (Luke 1:38). Tell God that you want to be as quick as Mary to respond saying, "Your will be done, Lord, and not my own."

Say boldly: "He went a little farther and fell on His face, and prayed, saying, 'O My Father, if it is possible, let this cup pass from Me; nevertheless, not as I will, but as *You* will'" (Matthew 26:39).

Pray powerfully: Lord, I want Your will and not mine to be done in my life. Show me what Your will is each day as I seek You for it. Give me a heart that says, "Not my will but Yours be done."

17. Tell Someone What God Has Done for You

It is wise to keep in mind everything God has done for you. It proves you have the fear of the Lord—reverence for God—in your heart. That way, you will "always be ready to give a defense to everyone who asks you a reason for the hope that is in you, with meekness and fear" (1 Peter 3:15). This is a powerful principle. "All men shall fear, and shall *declare the work of God; for they shall wisely consider His doing*" (Psalm 64:9). It is wise to not keep the great things God has done for us to ourselves. The Bible says, "Only fear the LORD, and serve Him in truth with all your heart; for *consider what great things He has done for you*" (1 Samuel 12:24). *Our love for God* gives us the courage to serve Him by sharing with others the amazing things He has done for us.

Say boldly: "Come and hear, all you who fear God, and I will declare what He has done for my soul" (Psalm 66:16).

Pray powerfully: Lord, help me to keep in mind and wisely consider all You have done for me. Teach me how to consider and declare Your works and tell others how You have specifically blessed me.

18. Forgive Others, and Make No Plans for Revenge

God gives us no leeway as far as forgiveness goes. Jesus laid down His life for us in a torturous way so that we can be completely forgiven of all our sins. He expects us to release others by forgiving them completely so we can move on with our lives. This is an unbendable and unbreakable rule. We were not made to carry unforgiveness without it slowly killing us. Revenge is even worse. It destroys us quickly. God says if we harbor revenge in our heart, He will not listen to our prayers. That means our relationship with Him doesn't grow until we get that out of our heart.

Revenge is never a good thing to have in your heart and mind, even when you believe another person deserves it. So don't go there. Revenge brings such anxiety into your mind and soul that it will negatively affect your health. Actually, the best revenge is to release that person completely into the Lord's hands. That way you don't forever keep that person attached to your life, even if it's only in your thoughts. It can be a terrifying thing to fall into the hands of God when someone has done evil to one of His children. God said,

"Vengeance is mine," and He means it (Deuteronomy 32:35). You want to get out of His way when that happens. He doesn't need your help.

Say boldly: "Whenever you stand praying, if you have anything against anyone, forgive him, that your Father in heaven may also forgive you your trespasses" (Mark 11:25).

Pray powerfully: Lord, help me not to live in unforgiveness and bitterness toward anyone. I know this is in total opposition to the way You want us to live. Enable me, instead, to forgive anyone who has hurt, neglected, or abused me or my family in any way. I don't want to forever hold that person to my life by not forgiving. I don't want to experience the torture that not forgiving someone can bring to me. Most of all, I don't want to delay Your forgiving me as you wait for me to obey You by forgiving others. Help me to be kind, tenderhearted, and forgiving, just as You forgave me (Ephesians 4:32).

19. Choose to Not Sit in Judgment of Others

When we make it a habit to constantly sit in judgment on other people, it's a sign of pride and arrogance on our part and calls greater judgment down on ourselves. That's because it's hypocritical to think we are without fault and therefore have the right to judge others. I am not saying we don't condemn sin when we see it. But critical judgment begins with ourselves. Jesus said, "Judge not, that you be not judged...And why do you look at the speck in your brother's eye, but do not consider the plank in your own eye?" (Matthew 7:1,3).

Jesus said to someone who referred to Him as good, "Why do you call Me good? No one is good but One, that is, God" (Luke 18:19). If Jesus did not think of Himself as good, then how can we ever think of ourselves that way? Jesus was sinless. We are not. Even if we do everything right, we still have thoughts and attitudes and unforgiveness that can creep in on us—especially when we think we have already conquered all that. It's only the righteousness of Jesus in us that makes us appear righteous before God. How can we sit in judgment of others?

Say boldly: "With what judgment you judge, you will be judged; and with the measure you use, it will be measured back to you" (Matthew 7:2).

Pray powerfully: Lord, show me where I am pridefully sitting in judgment on others and entertaining a critical spirit. I know criticizing others does not bring the peace and blessing I desire from You. Show me my own faults so that I can concentrate on getting rid of them and becoming more like You.

20. Give to God and Others So You Store Up Treasures in Heaven

God requires that we give to Him. If we recognize that everything we have was given to us by Him, it's easier to give a portion of it back to Him for the work of His kingdom. This is very important. Jesus said we cannot serve two masters—God and money—because we will love only one of them. (See Matthew 6:24.) Jesus also said, "Give to him who asks you, and from him who wants to borrow from you do not turn away" (Matthew 5:42). God wants us to not only *give* to Him, but also to give to others. "Blessed is he who considers the poor; the Lord will deliver him in time of trouble" (Psalm 41:1).

Say boldly: "Do not lay up for yourselves treasures on earth, where moth and rust destroy and where thieves break in and steal; but *lay up for yourselves treasures in heaven*, where neither moth nor rust destroys and where thieves do not break in and steal. For *where your treasure is, there your heart will be* also" (Matthew 6:19-21).

Pray powerfully: Lord, I know You love a "cheerful giver" (2 Corinthians 9:7). Your Word says, "The generous soul will be made rich, and he who waters will also be watered himself" (Proverbs 11:25). Help me to be cheerful and rich in generosity. And Your Word says, "He who gives to the poor will not lack, but he who hides his eyes will have many curses" (Proverbs 28:27). Show me exactly whom to give to and what to give. Help me to never rob You by failing to give You what You require.

Prayer Power

Lord, help me to do the things I need to do in my life so that whenever I feel afraid, I will have a strong foundation in You already established. I commit my life to You and everything in it. I praise You and thank You for who You are and all You have done for me. Help me to keep my mind focused on good things and not negative and frightening things.

Help me to always walk in Your ways and keep Your laws and commandments. Keep me from doing anything that compromises my walk with You. "Cause me to hear Your lovingkindness in the morning, for in You do I trust; cause me to know the way in which I should walk, for I lift up my soul to You" (Psalm 143:8).

Help me to easily share with others all the good things You have done in my life. Enable me to do the right things and *stop* doing the things that are not good for my life. Help me to forgive when I need to forgive and not hold on to thoughts of vengeance. Help me to get rid of all temptation to do otherwise. Show me anything I need to stop doing because it is not Your best for my life. Teach me to share the good things You have done for me with others who need to hear it. Enable me to give to You and to others in the way You want me to. Help me to do what I need to do to keep fear away from my life.

In Jesus' name I pray.

WORD POWER

I can do all things through Christ who strengthens me.

PHILIPPIANS 4:13

Whatever you do in word or deed,
do all in the name of the Lord Jesus,
giving thanks to God the Father through Him.

COLOSSIANS 3:17

Put off, concerning your former conduct,
the old man which grows corrupt
according to the deceitful lusts,
and be renewed in the spirit of your mind,
and... put on the new man which was
created according to God,
in true righteousness and holiness.

EPHESIANS 4:22-24

Bear one another's burdens,
and so fulfill the law of Christ.

GALATIANS 6:2

Come to Me, all you who labor and are heavy laden,
and I will give you rest.

MATTHEW 11:28

8

What Are the Enemy's Fear Tactics?

Jesus described Satan as His enemy. And God's enemy is our enemy. That's because the enemy hates anyone who believes in Jesus and worships the one true God. Those who do the bidding of our enemy hate us as well.

Extreme fear will always be one of the main tactics of our enemy. He will use evil means to promote fear and will do anything to makes us afraid. Our fear is the enemy's victory. Peace and freedom from fear will always be the gift God gives us. God does not want us to live in fear because fear of the enemy can destroy us. David prayed, "Hear my voice, O God, in my meditation; *preserve my life from fear of the enemy*" (Psalm 64:1).

If we are not aware that we have an enemy, and who that enemy is and what his tactics are, we will be manipulated, lied to, robbed, taken advantage of, and eventually witness his plans for our destruction as they manifest in our lives. One of the reasons Jesus came to earth was to destroy the works of the enemy. "He who sins is of the devil, for the devil has sinned from the beginning. *For this purpose the Son of God was manifested, that He might destroy the works of the devil*" (1 John 3:8). Jesus gave us a way to take back everything the enemy has stolen from us. In order to do that, we need to identify and be aware of the enemy's fear tactics and have some tactics of our own to resist him.

The Enemy's Tactic Is to Steal, Kill, and Destroy

The enemy wants to steal from you. He will rob you of your hope, your peace, and your faith in God if he is allowed to do so. He wants you to constantly live in fear. Something of our life is always stolen from us when we are afraid. When we are fearful, we let good opportunities slip by—we *don't* do things we *need* to do, and we *do* things we *shouldn't* do. Fear not only robs us of our joy, but it also robs us of our sleep and sense of well-being. Jesus said of our enemy, "The *thief* does not come except to *steal*, and to *kill*, and to *destroy. I have come that they may have life*, and that they may have it more abundantly" (John 10:10).

The enemy will devise ways to kill everything about you. He will try to kill your body, mind, marriage, aspirations, relationships, sense of purpose, and much more. The enemy not only wants us dead—unless, of course, we can be used by him for *his* purposes—he also wants the same for our children. Keep that in mind, and resist all enemy attacks on any part of your life or your family.

The enemy wants to destroy everything good in your life. He will try to destroy your health, family, work, finances, reputation, and love of God. Too many believers are being knocked around by the enemy of their soul and their life because they think bad things just happen to them and that's the way life is. So they are not actively engaged against the enemy, and as a result are totally unprepared to face his opposition.

Often our greatest battles involve keeping our family relationships strong—between siblings, parents, children, husband and wife, or in-laws. The enemy hates that we can be part of a family. He has to recruit others to his side with lies. Too many people don't understand that and play right into his hand by being unloving, cruel, selfish, and inconsiderate to their family members. They allow family bonds to be destroyed because they think they have the right to do so. They facilitate the enemy's plans. The battle for our family relationships is one we must win. And that requires ongoing prayer—not only during trying times, but also in advance of them.

The Enemy's Tactic Is to Devour

"Devour" means to swallow up ravenously. Did you know you can have a mind devoured by fear? Fear can render you incapacitated. That's how the enemy works. You may feel as if some parts of your life—or perhaps everything in your life—is being swallowed up, such as your finances, the results of all your hard work, your sense of purpose, your gifts, and your direction. This can make you feel as if all energy, motivation, sense of purpose, and anything else that sustains life and causes it to be worth living is being eaten away because of fear—even to the point of draining your faith and commitment to the Lord. If so, just know that you can put a stop to that and erect an invisible barrier against the enemy's attempts to devour your life.

The Bible says, "Be sober, be vigilant; because *your adversary the devil walks about like a roaring lion, seeking whom he may devour*" (1 Peter 5:8). We need to think clearly about what the enemy wants to devour of our life and be vigilant in prayer asking God to put a stop to it. We are instructed in the Bible to take God's kingdom by force. Part of that has to do with praying powerfully to God and taking back what the enemy has devoured.

The Enemy's Tactic Is to Entice
People to Believe His Lies

The enemy's greatest ploy is to blind people to the truth and deceive them with lies. He can do anything he wants to those who believe him and not God. That's why we must gain a solid knowledge of *God's truth*. When we cannot distinguish between God's truth and a lie of the enemy, we are in trouble.

The enemy is not everywhere. He can only be where there is an opening for him. The enemy doesn't know everything, and he doesn't know what you think. He only knows what you *say*. So watch what you say. If you say, "I hate my life, and I don't want to live anymore," the enemy will help you get what you say you want. Or if you say, "I know I can do all things through Christ who strengthens me, and God will enable me to live the life He has for me because I pray in Jesus' name," the enemy is powerless against your prayers in Jesus' name and can do nothing. The enemy is not even close to being as powerful as God. Only God is everywhere and all-powerful. Keep that firmly in your mind.

To prove that the enemy doesn't know everything, the "god of this age"—Satan, along with his demons—didn't understand what God's plan was by allowing Jesus to be crucified on the cross. That's because God's mysteries are not revealed to the enemy. The enemy's knowledge of the plans of God is limited. *"God has revealed them to us through His Spirit.* For the Spirit searches all things, yes, the deep things of God...no one knows the things of God except the Spirit of God"* (1 Corinthians 2:10-11). We have God's Holy Spirit in us, and He enables us to understand things unbelievers cannot. *"We have received, not the spirit of the world, but the Spirit who is from God, that we might know the things that have been freely given to us by God"* (1 Corinthians 2:12).

What a wonderful gift that we can know the truth that sets us free and reject the lies of the enemy that causes doubt.

People who themselves tell lies give a piece of their heart to the enemy every time they do so. We must decide to be people of the truth. That means believing and speaking only the truth. Nothing less.

Jesus said of Satan, "He was a murderer from the beginning, and does not stand in the truth, because there is no truth in him. When he speaks a lie, he speaks from his own resources, for *he is a liar and the father of it*" (John 8:44). Don't align yourself with the father of lies. Align yourself with the "Father of lights" and His Holy Spirit of truth (James 1:17).

The Enemy's Tactic Is to Bring Condemnation

If you truly walk according to the Spirit—being fully Spirit led— you will not sin against God. "*There is therefore now no condemnation to those who are in Christ Jesus, who do not walk according to the flesh, but according to the Spirit*" (Romans 8:1). But if you do violate one of God's laws and ways, He gives you the gifts of confession and repentance so you can clear the slate with Him right away. If you don't get rid of guilt, the enemy will pour condemnation on you, and you will not have peace or feel good about yourself or your life.

Jesus took care of condemnation so you don't have to live under that curse. You are no longer separated from God. (See Ephesians 4:8-10.) Jesus has broken the enemy's ability to keep you in captivity because of sin. So don't allow the enemy to push a lie on you that says, "You are guilty. You don't deserve to succeed in life." If you have received Jesus, you have been forgiven of all past sins. And you can decide to get free of subsequent sins by bringing them before God with a repentant heart and a full confession.

There is a great deal of fear in the heart of many people because of the ever-visible, overwhelming force of horrendous plans of the enemy being carried out because of lies believed by the deceived, who do his bidding. But the Bible says to believers in the one true God, "In righteousness you shall be established; *you shall be far from oppression, for you shall not fear; and from terror, for it shall not come near you*" (Isaiah 54:14). Determine to rely on the truth that sets you free and not the lies that cause destruction.

Determine to pray about everything that causes fear in your mind and heart.

Our focus must be on God and not our enemy, but that doesn't mean we ignore the enemy and pretend we don't have one. That would reveal our ignorance and lack of knowledge of God's truth. The enemy loves it when we are clueless. In order to combat his tactics, we need to have unfailing tactics of our own. Below are some of those tactics we cannot neglect to do.

To Combat the Enemy's Tactics, Realize You Are Already in the War

As a believer, you are already involved in spiritual warfare whether you realize it or not. You may think that some of the difficult things that happen to you or to others, or that are evident in situations in the world around you, are just the way life is and beyond your ability to do anything to affect them. But the situation is far more sinister than that. It's the result of *planning* by the enemy. You may believe you are not in any war, but you are.

Even if you have *not* yet received Jesus, you are still in the war. It's just that you are unaware of all that and therefore have no control over the things that happen to you. You could be suffering with frequently reoccurring problems—such as repeated illnesses, accidents, financial struggles, relationship problems, or whatever else—and you may think it's just bad luck, but it's not. It's the enemy of your soul—that you don't know you have—and you don't realize your foundation has been built on sand instead of the Rock.

We cannot afford the luxury of foolishly thinking, *If I don't acknowledge that I have an enemy, then I won't ever have to engage with the enemy.* The truth is, the enemy has a plan for your life and so does God. God gives you a *free will* and allows you to *choose His plan* in your life. Or not. Your choice determines your future.

I have known people who believed if they never acknowledged that the enemy exists—and especially if they don't allow for the fact that *God's* enemy is *their* enemy as well—then they can stay out of the war completely. But those who deny the spiritual war that is happening until the Lord returns are destined to lose it.

Even believers who *do* understand the enemy's warfare against us often think that when they contend in prayer for the will of the Lord to prevail in a specific battle, that once that battle is won, the war is over. *But the war is never over because the enemy never relents in his warfare against you.*

If we realize we are already in the war, we will be more able to stand strongly against the enemy in prayer. When Jesus died on the cross, He assured us of our victory over the enemy. But we still must wage the battle in prayer. *Prayer is the actual battle.* Our battlefield is our prayer closet or wherever we are praying. Prayer and God's Word are our first lines of defense in the battle against our enemy.

I wrote an entire book on this subject called *Prayer Warrior,* and in it I describe what a prayer warrior is. I said that although you may not think of yourself as a prayer warrior, if you are suffering, or *you see others suffering,* and you want to do something about it, you have the heart of a prayer warrior. *If you are incensed by injustice in your life, or in the lives of others,* and you would like to put an end to that, then you have the heart of a prayer warrior. *If you have you ever deeply wished you could have done something that might have prevented a tragedy*, then you have the heart of a prayer warrior.

In the Bible, when Jesus said, "Follow Me," He was in essence saying, "Come out of the world and into the kingdom of God." "Come out of danger and into safety." "Come out of the darkness and into the light." "Come out of stress and fear, and into peace." He said specifically, "Come to Me, all you who labor and are heavy laden, and *I will give you rest.* Take My yoke upon you and learn from Me, for I am gentle and lowly in heart, and *you will find rest for your souls. For My yoke is easy and My burden is light"* (Matthew 11:28-30*).* When you align yourself with God and rest in Him, even in the face of an enemy attack, then as you pray, the burdens you have in your heart will be laid upon Him. And the things He wants you to do for Him are made easier because *He* does the heavy lifting.

To Combat the Enemy's Tactics, Depart from Evil

Departing from evil means once you recognize you are in a spiritual war between God and His enemy, then you do all you can to make sure you are not giving the enemy any ground in your life.

Departing from evil means you walk with and live for God and not the world's idols. The Bible says, "The fear of the Lord, that is wisdom, and to *depart from evil is understanding"* (Job 28:28). People who do not have fear and reverence of God have no godly wisdom or understanding. God wants us to "abstain from every form of evil" (1 Thessalonians 5:22). People without the wisdom and understanding that come from God can easily allow some form of evil into their life where if they were completely sold out to God, they wouldn't.

The Bible says, "Let love be without hypocrisy. *Abhor what is evil.* Cling to what is good" (Romans 12:9). If we don't abhor what is evil and yet we claim to love God, we are hypocrites. The remedy for that is to *cling to what is good.*

God and His ways are always good.

To reiterate something we can't hear too often, we cannot have one foot in God's kingdom and one foot in the enemy's realm. Our lives have to be established on the Rock. The Bible says, "No other foundation can anyone lay than that which is laid, which is Jesus Christ" (1 Corinthians 3:11). We are advised to "choose none of [the oppressor's] ways" (Proverbs 3:31). We have to be diligent about this. It's too easy to choose our oppressor's ways when we can't identify him.

Jesus said, "Whoever comes to Me, and hears My sayings and does them, I will show you whom he is like: He is like a man building a house, who dug deep and *laid the foundation on the rock.* And when the flood arose, the stream beat vehemently against that house, and *could not shake it, for it was founded on the rock*" (Luke 6:47-48).

The solid Rock is Jesus. His presence in your life affects every aspect of it. The solid Rock—Jesus—is also called "The Word of God" (Revelation 19:13). Jesus and His Word are inseparable. It's on that solid foundation that we recognize and depart from evil. That means living the way God tells us to live. "Whoever listens to me will dwell safely, and will be secure, without fear of evil" (Proverbs 1:33). The "me" in this verse is wisdom.

To Combat the Enemy's Tactics, Rely on the Holy Spirit's Empowerment

Jesus told His disciples that after He was crucified and had risen again, He would go to His Father and send the Holy Spirit to be *with* them and *in* them. (See John 16:5-11.) The same is true for us today. When we receive Jesus, He gives us His Spirit to dwell in us.

It's the sign that we belong to Him. That is why we have to acknowledge the power of the Holy Spirit working *in* us and *through* us.

This next section of Scripture is so important it needs to be repeated here in this chapter on spiritual warfare, because if we don't get this, we will lose many battles. The Bible says, *"You are not in the flesh but in the Spirit, if indeed the Spirit of God dwells in you. Now if anyone does not have the Spirit of Christ, he is not His"* (Romans 8:9). If you do not have the Holy Spirit in you—He is also called the Spirit of Christ—then you are in the flesh because you have not received Jesus. Again, I am not talking about various outpourings or manifestations of the Holy Spirit. I am taking about what automatically happens when you receive the Lord.

When you received Jesus, *"you were sealed with the Holy Spirit of promise"* (Ephesians 1:13). The Holy Spirit in us "is *the guarantee of our inheritance*," which means our inheritance from God is a done deal (Ephesians 1:14). A big part of our inheritance from God is victory over our enemy.

The Spirit of Christ is the *power* of *God.* The Bible says, "The message of the cross is foolishness to those who are perishing, but *to us who are being saved it is the power of God"* (1 Corinthians 1:18). God shares His power with you. Your prayers have power because of His Holy Spirit living in you. God's Word has power, and the Holy Spirit brings it alive to you. That is the way He gives you power over the enemy. If you deny the Holy Spirit in you, you deny the power of God working through you. What Jesus accomplished on the cross is the grounds upon which we are saved. The resurrection of Jesus was always *God's plan*, and it destroyed the enemy's plans and all of his power.

This means when you receive the Lord, you are transported into a new kingdom, and you don't ever have to live in the realm of darkness again. Jesus came into this world as a light so that we who believe in Him don't have to live in the dark. (See John 12:46.) We are not only going to spend eternity with Him, but we are going to reign with Him in this life as well. This all happens by the power of the Holy Spirit in us. Jesus is "*not weak toward you, but mighty in you*" (2 Corinthians 13:3). Jesus is mighty in you by the power of His Spirit in you.

Jesus rules in your life, and the evil one does not. But you have to live as if you believe that. You don't want to be "traitors, headstrong, haughty, lovers of pleasure rather than lovers of God, *having a form of godliness but denying its power*" (2 Timothy 3:4-5). You don't want to have even the *appearance* of godliness but denying its power. The Bible says to stay away from people who do that.

To Combat the Enemy's Tactics, Know That Only the Lord Is Holy

Moses sang a song to the Lord to thank Him for delivering the Israelites. He said, "Who is like You, O LORD, among the gods? Who is like You, *glorious in holiness*, fearful in praises, doing wonders?" (Exodus 15:11).

Hannah thanked God for giving her the child she prayed for, saying, "*No one is holy like the LORD, for there is none besides You, nor is there any rock like our God*" (1 Samuel 2:2).

The victorious redeemed in heaven sang a song like the one Moses sang, and in the book of Revelation it's called the song of the Lamb. "Who shall not fear You, O Lord, and glorify Your name? *For You alone are holy*" (Revelation 15:4).

Now, this is something personal for me, but I believe it is from the Lord. I'm bothered when I hear someone say, "Holy _____!" (Fill in the blank with whatever word you have heard people use.) Regardless of whether it's filled in with something innocuous or something obscene, it disturbs me. When I hear that, I always say to myself, "There is none holy like the Lord." Sometimes I say it aloud because I can't help myself. For example, when someone says, "Holy cow," my first thought is *idol worship*. And I say, "There is none holy like the Lord." I myself have never said "Holy (anything)." It has never been an exclamation that appealed to me in any way. I never thought much about it when other people said it, except it made no sense why anyone would. But I believe God put this truth in my heart, and now I understand why those exclamations are so mindless and irritating to me.

To exalt such profane, mundane, and, in many cases, crass things above the Lord is not pleasing to Him. And we don't want to displease God. It's not respectful to Him, so it doesn't demonstrate the fear of God. Therefore, it cannot be good for our health and well-being. It's one of many lies the enemy encourages.

We always have to be thinking of whose kingdom we are planted in. This is not legalism. This is a condition of the heart that reflects whose kingdom I have chosen. I know that if it grieves my spirit to hear that, it grieves the Holy Spirit even more. If you do that, ask God what He thinks about it and if He feels it's glorifying to Him. And if you feel brave when you hear someone else use this profane comment, you can say, "There is none holy like the Lord." You are not preaching. You are just making a statement of fact. And I am not telling you what to do. I am simply making a point about being aware of what kingdom you are in.

People who are influenced by the enemy are those who have given him a place in their lives, either deliberately or out of ignorance. Jesus is Lord, and we can't water that down in our mind or heart in any way. God dwells in us by His Spirit, and we must never submit to any other, nor should we demean Him—even if that is done mindlessly.

To Combat the Enemy's Tactics, Go to Battle in Prayer

Too many believers have been deceived by the enemy into thinking either that they don't need to pray or that their prayers are powerless. Neither one of these statements is true. God gives us a free will, and we are judged by what we choose to do in response to what He says. God requires that we pray fervently and unceasingly. Don't think that the enemy can't win some battles if we neglect to do what God instructs us to do. He can and he will.

What peace and confidence we can have when we realize that *our ability to pray in power comes from God.* "Not that we are sufficient of ourselves to think of anything as being from ourselves, but *our sufficiency is from God*" (2 Corinthians 3:5). We pray as He leads us by His Spirit. That's why you must recognize that you always have the Holy Spirit in you, so you do not have to let the enemy bully you with fear that your prayers are not strong enough against his opposition.

Jesus didn't pray that His followers would be taken out of the world to protect them, but that God would "*keep them from the evil one*" (John 17:15). He said, "They are not of the world, just as I am not of the world. Sanctify them by Your truth. Your word is truth" (John 17:16-17).

That means if you have received Jesus as your Savior, the enemy's power in your life has been annihilated. He can only convince you with his lies to doubt God's Word and all that Jesus accomplished. If you hold fast to God speaking to you through His Word, and through His Holy Spirit in you, you will know how to pray, and you will have power over the enemy for the rest of your life.

God desires "that you may become blameless and harmless, children of God without fault in the midst of a crooked and perverse generation, among whom you shine as lights in the world" (Philippians 2:15). That doesn't happen without prayer.

You have to know who your enemy is and what his intentions are. You have to know God is always good and the enemy is always evil. You don't need to dwell on the enemy's evil deeds except as the Holy Spirit makes you aware of something for which He wants you to pray. You do need to focus on God's goodness and thank Him for it every day. The Bible says to "be wise in what is good, and simple concerning evil. And *the God of peace will crush Satan under your feet shortly*" (Romans 16:19-20). Trust God's Word to your heart.

When you pray, keep in mind that God is all-powerful. Through the cross, Jesus destroyed the rule on earth of principalities and powers of evil (Colossians 2:15). He did not destroy *them*, but He did destroy their *power to torment* those who have His Holy Spirit in them.

God's power is without limit. The enemy's power is limited. The only way the enemy has power is because people give it to him by believing his lies.

After God made a way for the Israelites to escape slavery under the Egyptians, He gave His people manna to eat every day. But in response to what God gave them, they complained and wanted what they craved and not what He provided for them. After all the astounding miracles He did for them, they still did not obey Him. "*They did not remember His power*: The day when He redeemed them from the enemy" (Psalm 78:42). If you ever think the enemy is as powerful as God, then you are subject to his plans for you. Our victory comes when we focus on the all-powerful strength of our Lord God for whom nothing is impossible.

To Combat the Enemy's Tactics, Exert the Authority Jesus Gave You

When you received Jesus, you became a new person, so the enemy cannot throw your past in your face. He can't say to you, "Look at all the things you did. You have no authority over me." The Bible says, "*If anyone is in Christ, he is a new creation*; old things have passed away; behold, all things have become new" (2 Corinthians 5:17). Say this verse out loud and then add, "I am a new creation. The past is gone, and I have been made new."

Don't let the enemy tell you that you have no right to pray and expect God to answer because you are imperfect or you've failed. Those words are not God giving you revelation for your life. They are words from the enemy of your soul wanting to discourage, demean, and destroy you. If you have unconfessed sin in your life, repent of it and confess it before God. Then thank God that your authority in prayer does not depend on your being perfect. It's because of what Jesus perfectly accomplished on the cross, and *He* is perfect. When the enemy tries to bring you down, bring *him* down instead with praise and worship to the Lord. The enemy hates that.

Jesus said, "All authority has been given to Me in heaven and on earth" (Matthew 28:18). He also said He has given us authority "*over all the power of the enemy*" (Luke 10:19). Because you have received Jesus and have *His Spirit* in your heart, your prayers have power in Jesus' name. Jesus is mighty in you because His Spirit is in you. It says of Jesus that "though He was crucified in weakness, yet *He lives by the power of God. For we also are weak in Him, but we shall live with Him by the power of God*" (2 Corinthians 13:4). We may *feel* weak, but this is not about us. It's about *Him*. He is powerful, and His Spirit is in us. It's a done deal.

God has made the name of Jesus to be far greater than any other name. "*God also has highly exalted Him and given Him the name which is above every name,* that *at the name of Jesus every knee should bow,* of those in heaven, and of those on earth, and of those under the earth, and that every tongue should confess that Jesus Christ is Lord, to the glory of God the Father" (Philippians 2:9-11).

If you can anchor in your mind and heart the full significance of Jesus' giving you authority to use His name in prayer, it can change your life and save the lives of others for whom you pray.

The Holy Spirit in us is the proof of our authority in prayer. Paul said, "*No one can say that Jesus is Lord except by the Holy Spirit*" (1 Corinthians 12:3). The Holy Spirit in us is the proof that we are God's. By Him God *establishes* us, *anoints* us, and *seals* us. "He who *establishes us* with you in Christ and has *anointed us* is God, who also has *sealed us* and *given us the Spirit in our hearts as a guarantee*" (2 Corinthians 1:21-22).

We have been given the authority to stand in prayer against the evil powers of darkness that want to wage war against the kingdom of God and His people. The truth is, we question the authority Jesus has given us when we don't pray in His name. Jesus has given us a key to His kingdom, and we don't use it to unlock the door. Don't allow the enemy to cause you to question, even for a moment, the authority you have in Jesus' name.

The Bible says, God has "*delivered us from the power of darkness and conveyed us into the kingdom of the Son* of His love, in whom we have redemption through His blood, the forgiveness of sins" (Colossians 1:13-14).

The word "conveyed" in terms of war has to do with an army that has been captured and sent to another place—often from one country to another. Jesus captured us from the kingdom of darkness and conveyed us to His kingdom of light. We have been transferred out of enemy territory and into God's kingdom. That happened the moment we received Jesus.

However, God's plan for us is not just one deliverance and done. It says of the Lord that *He is the one* "*who delivered us* from so great a death, and *does deliver us*; in whom we trust that *He will still deliver us*" (2 Corinthians 1:10). *Our battle for freedom against the enemy is ongoing, and so our prayers must be ongoing as well. Remember always that* prayer *is* the battle. And our authority is in Jesus' name.

To Combat the Enemy's Tactics, Don't Drift Away from the Truth

Before I came to the Lord, I was searching into a number of occult practices and religions, trying to find a way to God. One of those false religions believed there was no such thing as evil in the world because evil only exists in your mind. So if you get rid of all evil in your mind, then there would be no evil in your life. That is totally wrong! That concept doesn't work *at all.* Talk about believing a lie. It was a popular religion in Hollywood at the time that used Christian terms to mean something different than what they were intended to mean. The deceiver himself was the author of that religion. If the deceiver can get us to believe that lie, then he can do whatever he wants in our life and make us think it's a good idea.

The Bible says, "Do not be overcome by evil, but overcome evil with good" (Romans 12:21). God's Word is good. So speaking it and sharing it is good. That's because God is good and this is His truth. We have to know His truth so well that we can instantly spot a lie of the enemy.

The Bible says, "*Who is a liar but he who denies that Jesus is the Christ?* He is antichrist who denies the Father and the Son. Whoever denies the Son does not have the Father either; he who acknowledges the Son has the Father also" (1 John 2:22-23). You must know this with complete certainty.

Do you ever wonder how *you*, as a believer, can see God's truth so clearly, but there are those who cannot see it at all? It happens because at some point in time they *chose* to reject God's truth and believe a lie they wanted to believe. So they were given over to deceiving spirits of the enemy. This is not just a temporary condition until they come to their senses. This is a major stronghold that will take major deliverance by the Deliverer, requiring great awakening, repentance, and confession on the part of the deceived. (See 1 Timothy 4:1-2.)

God has set it up that we have a will, and we decide what we *will* or *will not* do. Will we strengthen ourselves in His Word so it becomes a spiritual weapon against the realm of darkness? Will we align *our* will with *God's* will in order to see the enemy pushed back? The enemy wants to distract you, deceive you, discourage you, and destroy you so that God's promises for your life will never be realized.

Don't allow your heart to drift away from the things of God, because it surely will. We're all like that. Our nature is selfish. We drift toward self-focus and away from self-sacrifice unless we deliberately focus on God every day. "We must give the more earnest heed to the things we have heard, *lest we drift away*" (Hebrews 2:1).

The Word of God is living, so you can live in it and let it live in you. The Word of God was inspired by the Holy Spirit, and when we read it, the Holy Spirit makes it alive in our heart. He breathes greater understanding into our spirit. Our eyes are opened to spiritual understanding we did not have as unbelievers. The Word of God is powerful and "sharper than any two-edged sword, piercing even to the division of soul and spirit, and of joints and marrow, and *is a discerner of the thoughts and intents of the heart*" (Hebrews 4:12).

The Word of God will reveal discrepancies between your soul and spirit, in case your spirit wants to obey God and your soul does not.

God knows when we are drifting away from the truth and compromising our walk with Him. Jesus was talking to His disciples about evil men who would persecute them, and He said, "Do not fear them. *For there is nothing covered that will not be revealed,* and hidden that will not be known" (Matthew 10:26). In other words, God sees the evil that men think and do. We can't hide anything from God because He knows everything and sees everything. "There is no creature hidden from His sight, but all things are naked and open to the eyes of Him to whom we must give account" (Hebrews 4:13). That is a sobering thought.

To Combat the Enemy's Tactics, Resist Him

Sometimes we can be so overwhelmed by what is happening in our lives that we do not see the enemy's part in the situation. And if we do see it, we may not know how to resist what he is doing. The Bible simply says, "*Submit to God. Resist the devil and he will flee from you*" (James 4:7). The way we submit to God is to spend time with Him in prayer, praise, and in His Word, and do everything He says. Joyfully. Wholeheartedly. Uncompromisingly.

But how do we resist the enemy?

Resisting the enemy means walking closely with God and knowing that "when the enemy comes in like a flood, the Spirit of the Lord will lift up a standard against him" (Isaiah 59:19). That is no small thing. The Spirit of the Lord, who is in you, knows what to do.

Resisting the enemy means refusing to be tempted away from the things of God. The enemy's plan is to lead you away from the truth and into temptation to not obey God. He does it with deception. Jesus instructed His disciples who were with Him every day to "*pray that you may not enter into temptation*" (Luke 22:40). We can all be tempted, and we should never think we are so secure in ourselves that we don't need to ask God to help us stand strong against temptation. "*Let him who thinks he stands take heed lest he fall*" (1 Corinthians 10:12). The Bible goes on to say, "No temptation has overtaken you except such as is common to man; but *God is faithful, who will not allow you to be tempted beyond what you are able, but with the temptation will also make the way of escape*, that you may be able to bear it" (1 Corinthians 10:13).

Resisting the enemy means refusing to spend time with people who act like the devil. We used to live in darkness before we received the Lord, but now we walk in the light (Ephesians 5:8). We must prove what kingdom we want to be in and "have no fellowship with the unfruitful works of darkness, but rather expose them" (Ephesians 5:11). Remember always that "we do not wrestle against flesh and blood, but *against principalities, against powers, against the rulers of the darkness of this age, against spiritual hosts of wickedness in the heavenly places*" (Ephesians 6:12).

Remember that "the *path of the just is like the shining sun, that shines ever brighter unto the perfect day. The way of the wicked is like darkness*; they do not know what makes them stumble" (Proverbs 4:18-19).

In the Bible, leaven in bread is an illustration of how sin can permeate our life if we don't stop it or bring it to an end. This is especially true when we spend time with people who do evil things unrepentantly. You can usually see who has a negative influence on your life or the lives of your children or spouse. For example, if you are around angry people who encourage you to be angry too, that is not a good situation. The Bible says, "Be angry, and do not sin: do *not let the sun go down on your wrath, nor give place to the devil*" (Ephesians 4:26-27). A connection is here between allowing anger to become a habit and giving the enemy a piece of your heart.

"Blessed is the man who endures temptation; for when he has been approved, *he will receive the crown of life* which the Lord has promised to those who love Him" (James 1:12).

Resisting the enemy means removing anything in our lives that we have allowed to become an idol. All idols are nothing in themselves. (See 1 Corinthians 8:4.) It's the demonic powers behind idols that are real and corrupting. We are never to give them a place in our lives in any way.

Resisting the enemy means worshipping and praising God as a way of life. When God delivered David from the hands of his enemy, he said, "*I will call upon the LORD, who is worthy to be praised; so shall I be saved from my enemies*" (2 Samuel 22:4). David said, "He sent from above, He took me, *He drew me out of many waters. He delivered me from my strong enemy*, from those who hated me; for they were too strong for me" (2 Samuel 22:17-18). At the first sign of the enemy's attack or encroachment, speak or sing praise to God. Worship Him wholeheartedly! It is one of the most powerful tactics against the enemy.

To Combat the Enemy's Tactics, Put On the Whole Armor of God

The Bible instructs us to "*put on the whole armor of God, that you may be able to stand against the wiles of the devil*" (Ephesians 6:11). That means there is spiritual armor we can choose to put on that will protect us from the plans of evil. (See Ephesians 6:11-18.) We have to do it every day. This is briefly what comprises our spiritual armor. We must:

Gird our waist with truth (verse 14). This means asking God to keep us undeceived. We know that "the whole world lies under the sway of the wicked one" (1 John 5:19). They foster lies, but we can know the truth that sets us free.

Put on the breastplate of righteousness (verse 14). The righteousness of Jesus covers your heart so the enemy cannot give you a mortal heart wound. Decide every day to live a life obedient to God, and ask His Holy Spirit to help you do that.

Shoe our feet with the preparation of the gospel of peace (verse 15). Soldiers always have to take care of their feet. You, too, have to have a solid foundation on which to stand. Jesus already prepared that for us. He has given us peace that is unimaginable in the midst of what we may experience. The enemy wants to steal your peace. Peace is the way you live because you received the Prince of Peace, and the Holy Spirit of peace lives in you.

Take the shield of faith in order to have the protection we need (verse 16). Faith dissolves our fear and gives us courage. Your faith in the God of the impossible means all things are possible for you because you believe.

Take the helmet of salvation that protects us from the enemy, who wants to blind us to all that Jesus accomplished on the cross (verse 17). Jesus gave us salvation when we received Him, but we need to understand fully what Jesus accomplished for us and who we really are in Christ.

Take the sword of the Spirit, which is the Word of God (verse 17). We cannot win any spiritual battle without God's Word. It's like a double-edged sword in our hands. It is a *defensive* and an *offensive* weapon. The Bible is much more than a history book. It's living and powerful.

Pray always and ongoingly (verse 18). This means praying about everything, and praying through problems until you see the answer. Be watchful at all times—frequently and consistently and constantly. Your delight is to do God's will, which pleases Him.

These are all protective spiritual weapons we don't want to be without. This is how we are armed *"with strength for the battle"*

(2 Samuel 22:40). This is how we "cast off the works of darkness" and "put on the armor of light" (Romans 13:12). This is so important, and it's well worth studying much further about the armor of God.

Moses told the Israelites before they crossed over the Jordan River that they would defeat the enemies they faced there. He said, *"Be strong and of good courage, do not fear nor be afraid of them; for the* LORD *your God, He is the One who goes with you. He will not leave you nor forsake you"* (Deuteronomy 31:6). We don't have to live in constant fear of the enemy if we let our fear draw us closer to God in prayer. He goes with *us* when we go with *Him*.

If you come under attack remember, "The Lord is the Spirit; and where the Spirit of the Lord is, there is liberty" (2 Corinthians 3:17). Seek the presence of the Lord immediately.

If it ever seems to you as if something is always coming along to defeat you, it's probably the enemy trying to wear you down and get you off the path of fulfilling God's plan for your life. Remember that no matter how bad things become, God is still on the throne. He always sees His high purpose for you and His plan for your life, even if you cannot see it at that moment. Keep in mind that you have an enemy who wants to steal your life. Don't allow that to happen. Become the prayer warrior God is calling you to be and fight for it.

Prayer Power

Thank You, Jesus, that You have made me an heir with You of all that our heavenly Father has for His children. Thank You for the great hope I have in You because You protect me from the enemy when I live Your way and pray according to Your will. Thank You for paying the ultimate price to win the war against your enemy and mine.

Lord, help me to build my life on the strength of my relationship with You and upon the solid rock of Your Word. Protect me from every lie of the enemy so that I'm never swayed from Your truth. Reveal to me any lies I have accepted as truth. Help me to depart from evil and never drift away from *Your* truth. I know that "though an army may encamp against me, my heart shall not fear" because You are with me (Psalm 27:3).

Enable me to always hear the voice of Your Holy Spirit leading me to pray and empowering me to stand strong against the enemy. Show me where my prayer is most needed for myself, my family, and the people and situations You put on my heart. Help me to not think of prayer as merely asking You to fix things, but rather as the way to do battle and take dominion over the works of darkness, as You have said to do.

Thank You for giving me authority to pray in Your name, Jesus, and to know You hear and will answer my prayers according to Your will. Help me to use the authority You have given me in prayer to advance Your kingdom on earth. Teach me how to put on the spiritual armor You have given me so that I and my loved ones and the people I care about are protected and prepared for any plan of the enemy to destroy us. Thank You, Lord, that You "will deliver me from every evil work and preserve me" for Your "heavenly kingdom" (2 Timothy 4:18). Deliver me "from fear of the enemy" (Psalm 64:1). In You, Lord, I have put my trust.

In Jesus' name I pray.

WORD POWER

When the enemy comes in like a flood,
the Spirit of the LORD will lift up a standard against him.

ISAIAH 59:19

The Lord is faithful, who will establish you
and guard you from the evil one.

2 THESSALONIANS 3:3

Blessed is the Lord God of Israel,
for He has visited and redeemed His people...
that we should be saved from our enemies and
from the hand of all who hate us...
to grant us that we, being delivered
from the hand of our enemies,
might serve Him without fear, in holiness and righteousness
before Him all the days of our life.

LUKE 1:68,71,74-75

By this I know that You are well pleased with me,
because my enemy does not triumph over me.

PSALM 41:11

The LORD is my light and my salvation; whom shall I fear?
The LORD is the strength of my life;
of whom shall I be afraid?...
Though an army may encamp against me,
my heart shall not fear.

PSALM 27:1,3

9

What Overcomes the
Fear of Death?

In my twenties I left college after my junior year to sing with several popular singing groups at that time. Those were opportunities I couldn't turn down. Between them all I traveled to nearly every state in the United States with the exception of Alaska and several of the New England states. We also went to England, France, South Africa, and Brazil. It was exciting to see places I'd heard of and read about.

During those years I was constantly on the road. But no matter how great each place was, I could have kissed the ground when I returned home to Los Angles and was back in my own apartment, in my own bed, going to familiar places, and spending time with my friends. Gradually, being home was more important to me than touring any foreign land could ever be.

I believe heaven will be like that. No matter how great our life has been here on earth, or how many things we loved about it, we will feel as though we are finally home when we go to be with the Lord and see the people we have loved who have gone before us.

In heaven we will have no fear, anxiety, worry, panic, sickness, or pain. We will certainly have no fear of death or what the future may hold. All the problems we had on earth will be gone, and there will be nothing to fear in our heavenly home.

Just as we all had a specific time and place of birth, so we will all have a specific time and place of death. We had no control over the situation coming into the world, and although our prayers have power, I don't know for certain if they can significantly influence our place, time, or manner of death. But I fully believe those last details of our life are well worth praying about.

However, we *do* have control over where we will end up the moment our body dies. If we have received Jesus, our future home will be with Him in heaven. So unless we turn our backs on God (our Creator and heavenly Father), and also Jesus (our Savior, Redeemer, Provider, Deliverer, Protector, and Friend), and reject God's Holy Spirit (who is the Spirit of love, peace, joy, comfort, truth, and power), Heaven is where we are going.

I'm certain Heaven is a real place, and that is why I capitalized it just now. We are going there one day—and not just to visit. It's a destination where we will live forever.

Jesus said, "No one can come to Me unless the Father who sent Me draws him; and *I will raise him up at the last day*" (John 6:44). Our Father God draws us to Himself, and Jesus raises us up on our last day on earth.

Because we have chosen to make our final home with Jesus in eternity, we can choose to prepare for our own transition from this life to the next. We do that by walking closely enough with God to hear Him speak to our heart and feel Him breathe life, strength, peace, and rest into our being. From what I have observed over the years, it appears that those who walked most closely with God had the greatest peace at the time of their departure from this world.

Those who kept bitterly clinging to life—even to the point of denying that they could ever die, up until the time they did—seemed to struggle the most. This is my limited experience, of course, but I've seen enough to believe there is something to it.

God allows suffering in our lives. We don't like that part, but He uses it to cause us to draw closer to Him. And it works. Because the closer we walk with God, the more peace we have about things that happen, including our time of departure. The sooner we can settle this issue with God—letting Him take away our fear and dread and give us peace about where we are ultimately going—the greater the peace is ahead for you and for the loved ones you leave behind.

The more clearly you can see heaven in your mind—the place Jesus talked about, and about which other men of God in the Bible wrote—the more peace you will have when the time comes to make that transition.

Having an idea of what heaven is like, based on God's Word, takes walking daily with God and learning more about what Jesus accomplished for you and why. It means being assured that His Holy Spirit in you will lead you home. He won't forget you. He won't leave you stranded. Even if you miss the mark of God's standards and get off the track He has for you, He will still give you a way back. It is called confession and repentance. It's saying with a repentant heart, "Lord, this is where I've been and what I've done. Please forgive me." And it's not because He doesn't know what you've been doing and needs to find out. He already knows. He wants to see that *you* recognize your errors and desire His forgiveness. He wants to hear you say, "Lord, I don't want to live my life without You. I want to be fully restored back to You and walk closely with You forever." God gives us this choice every day. Do we want to walk closely with Him or not?

There have been a number of people I have known well who in the last few years have died suddenly and, in my mind, prematurely.

It brought home clearly that we never know when our life may end. We can't wait until we think the end is near to get ready to meet the Lord in eternity. We must get ready now—and every day from now on. When we live that way, we aren't living in fear of death. And this is very important to our well-being. It's an issue we need to get settled in our mind and soul.

We need to know to whom we belong, and who is always with us, both now and forever. Below is a checklist to make sure you have done what you need to do in preparation for eternity so you don't have to live another day in fear of it.

Make Sure Your Name Is Written in the Lamb's Book of Life

Jesus did His part on the cross, and now you have to do yours. You have to receive Him and all that He accomplished. "Nor is there salvation in any other, for *there is no other name under heaven given among men by which we must be saved*" (Acts 4:12). Because I know that some people who are dying, or have a loved one who is dying, or they have a strong fear of death, will read this chapter first, I must say this again. God sent Jesus to suffer the consequences for our sins by His crucifixion on the cross. He died in our place so we don't have to ever be separated from God. He then rose from the dead—just as He said He would—and ascended into heaven to prepare the way for us to be with Him forever and have power over our enemy here on earth. He sent His Holy Spirit to live in us to comfort, guide, and help us become more like Him. We don't earn salvation. It is God's gift to us. "By grace *you have been saved through faith*, and that not of yourselves; *it is the gift of God*, not of works, lest anyone should boast" (Ephesians 2:8-9).

That means I'm not saved because I *am* such a good person, or I am *thinking* about being a good person, or one day I *know I will* be a good person. I'm saved when I recognize I can't be the kind of good person God wants me to be on my own, and I need the full forgiveness and redemption God has for me through Jesus Christ, His Son.

It's not enough to just be a good person who goes to church. Many people attend a Christian church, but they have not truly received Jesus as Lord and Savior. As a result, they do not have the Holy Spirit in them as their Helper, Comforter, and Guide.

"These things I have written to you who believe in the name of the Son of God, *that you may know that you have eternal life*, and that you may continue to believe in the name of the Son of God" (1 John 5:13). *You need to know without a doubt that you have eternal life ahead with God.* This is extremely important. This is something you have to do for yourself and also for others you care about. Don't hesitate because this determines where you will spend forever.

When we enter heaven, we will be in the presence of God, and the Holy Spirit of God will get us there. We are not just dangling out in space. We are anchored to God by His Holy Spirit in us. And *our names are written in the Lamb's Book of Life!*

This is very important.

The apostle John was given a great revelation from Jesus about what is ahead for believers. What Jesus revealed to John is written in the book of Revelation, the last book in the Bible. In it we are assured that if we have received Jesus, our names "*are written in the Lamb's Book of Life*" (Revelation 21:27).

John said regarding the end times, "I saw the dead, small and great, standing before God, and books were opened. And another book was opened, which is the Book of Life. And the dead were judged according to their works, by the things which were written in the books...And anyone *not found written in the Book of Life* was cast into the lake of fire" (Revelation 20:12,15).

The Bible tells us, "Do not love the world or the things in the world. If anyone loves the world, the love of the Father is not in him. For all that is in the world—the lust of the flesh, the lust of the eyes, and the pride of life—is not of the Father but is of the world. And the world is passing away, and the lust of it; but he *who does the will of God abides forever*" (1 John 2:15-17). This doesn't mean we can't live *in* the world. It means our greatest treasure is not in the world, and we don't buy into a godless worldview. It doesn't mean we can never make a mistake and walk outside of God's will. It means we don't intentionally stay outside of God's will once we understand what God's will is.

You can overcome the fear of death when you know for certain where you're going after you die.

Make sure your name is written in the Lamb's Book of Life. This cannot be seen by us, but God sees your name there. This is too crucial to neglect.

The most important thing to know about heaven is that you are going to be with the Lord forever, as well as with your loved ones who also have received Him. You don't have to know all the details. Just know it's going to be wonderful beyond anything you have ever imagined. Remember, you are not buying a house you have to pay for the rest of your life. You are being given a mansion for free that lasts forever. Let's not be picky.

Realize That Jesus Overcame Death and Hell for You

Everyone has a place they will go when they die. Some will be with God, and some will be separated from God. It's not a matter of God sending people to hell. It's a matter of where God is not present *is* hell. That's what hell is—the absence of God's presence. That's where people end up who reject Him. "These shall be punished with everlasting destruction from the presence of the Lord and from the glory of His power" (2 Thessalonians 1:9). This is not a threat or a promise. This is a statement of fact. People whose iniquity has not been paid for by the Lord will suffer for it in eternal separation from God. Jesus has prepared a wonderful place for those who are His. And neither death nor hell can separate them from Him. (See Hebrews 2:14-15.) This is not something to take lightly.

Jesus told His disciples they would be sad when He was gone, but they would be joyful knowing they would see Him again. Jesus said about His coming death, "You will weep and lament, but the world will rejoice; and you will be sorrowful, but your sorrow will be turned into joy...Therefore you now have sorrow; but *I will see you again and your heart will rejoice*, and *your joy no one will take from you*" (John 16:20,22).

The resurrection of Jesus proved He was who He said He was, and He did exactly what He said He would do.

Be Certain You Have a Clean Heart and a Right Spirit Within You

It's true that we don't have anything to do with the removal of all our sins from our record. That was taken care of when we received Him. "*He has not dealt with us according to our sins*, nor punished us according to our iniquities...as far *as the east is from the west, so far has He removed our transgressions from us*" (Psalm 103:10,12). But after we are born again in our spirit, when we sin again—or miss the mark God has for us—we must confess it to God in order to receive His forgiveness. If we don't, we will not receive all God has for us in this life. We need to keep current on that so we don't waste precious time while He waits for us to clear the slate with Him. God does not reward disobedience to His laws and ways.

God wants us to have a clean heart. A clean heart has no iniquity in it. Iniquity is unconfessed sin.

So it is not only a matter of calling Jesus "Lord." It is also a matter of doing what He says. Jesus said, "*Not everyone who says to Me, 'Lord, Lord,' shall enter the kingdom of heaven, but he who does the will of My Father in heaven.* Many will say to Me in that day, 'Lord, Lord, have we not prophesied in Your name, cast out demons in Your name, and done many wonders in Your name?' And then I will declare to them, 'I never knew you; depart from Me, you who practice lawlessness!'" (Matthew 7:21-23). That is not something we ever want to hear from God.

God wants us to have a right spirit. A right spirit fears God and wants to live God's way. We live God's way because we love Him and trust that His laws and ways are for our benefit because He loves us. Our desire is to be in His will.

There is no way to heaven outside of Jesus. The will of God for your life in general is found in God's Word. The will of God for the specifics of your life are found in prayer and in worship. God will speak to your heart in those times. Frequently ask Him to create in you a clean heart and renew a right spirit within you. You will never be in the will of God if you don't have both. Don't carry bitterness, anger, lack of forgiveness, mean thoughts, and unexpressed nastiness. You will not be free of fear—including the fear of death—if you are not in, or at least seeking, the will of God. This can happen the moment you surrender your life to Jesus. It's never too late to get right with God as long as you have breath within you.

Recall What the Bible Says About Death and Heaven

Jesus has prepared a place for us who love Him. He said, "Let not your heart be troubled; you believe in God, believe also in Me. *In My Father's house are many mansions*; if it were not so, I would have told you. *I go to prepare a place for you.* And if I go and prepare a place for you, I will come again and receive you to Myself; that where I am, there you may be also" (John 14:1-3).

In heaven we will rest in peace from our labor. "Blessed are the dead who die in the Lord from now on…that they may rest from their labors, and their works follow them" (Revelation 14:13).

Our bondage to the fear of death can keep us from doing what we need to do when we need to do it. But *Jesus released us from the fear of death.* Jesus gave His life "that through death He might destroy him who had the power of death, that is, the devil, and *release those who through fear of death were all their lifetime subject to bondage*" (Hebrews 2:14-15). Our fear of death can be a lifelong stumbling block to us.

Jesus consoled His followers who were being persecuted, saying, "Do not fear any of those things which you are about to suffer. Indeed, the devil is about to throw some of you into prison, that you may be tested, and you will have tribulation ten days. *Be faithful until death, and I will give you the crown of life*" (Revelation 2:10). There is great reward for those who are *killed specifically because they are Christians. The crown of life is no small compensation for faithfulness to the end.* Jesus said to His disciples, "Rejoice and be exceedingly glad, for great is your reward in heaven, for so they persecuted the prophets who were before you" (Matthew 5:12). That is a very hard pill to swallow. I believe that Jesus is with them when they are murdered for their faith in Him. And they have a special place in heaven near God's throne.

Few of us will die because we are believers in Christ. The point is, we will be with Him no matter what. Jesus has prepared a place for us. We don't have to be worried, fearful, anxious, or full of panic because we are not sure what the color scheme will be and if we will like the accommodations. We will be in the presence of God, and we will experience His love, peace, joy, and rest. And we will worship

Him continually forever because we will be eternally grateful. The best thing about the Garden of Eden was God's presence. The worst thing about it was the presence of the enemy. In heaven, the enemy will not be there.

Find Joy in Your Heart When Heaven Is Real in Your Mind

The more real heaven becomes to you, the better prepared you will be to go there. We will never know all the details until we get there, and we don't need to. We just have to know Jesus, who has reconciled us to God and given us His Spirit. He knows everything, and He has taken care of the accommodations. We can trust Him to do all He said He would. He said He has prepared a place for us with Him, and that that is really all we need to know. We need nothing more than to live in His presence and enjoy Him forever.

I remember the day I no longer feared death anymore. Even after I became a believer and knew what Jesus said about eternity, I still feared the process of dying. And although I had resolved what death meant as a daughter of God, I still was anxious about getting there. As a new believer, I seriously wondered, *What if I die and God doesn't remember me? How will I get to heaven if He forgets me?* I had felt forgotten and abandoned enough in my life that I had those horrible "What if?" thoughts. (Remember those from chapter 1?) When I asked God about that, He reminded me this was impossible because His Spirit dwelled within me. His Spirit will lead me home.

I read in the Bible that, "*Precious in the sight of the LORD is the death of His saints*" (Psalm 116:15). I love that. My death—and yours—is precious to God. He cares about that transition as much as we do. He will not leave us hanging in limbo, wondering if He sees or knows. That is not going to happen. That verse gave me great peace as well.

As I learned to pray about everything, I thought that because we can pray about everything in our lives, why can't we pray about death? After all, it is the most certain and inevitable part of life. So I have prayed about that for me and my loved ones. And I still do.

My own father gave me specific instructions about his death. He wanted to die at home—at the time he was living with me and my family—and he didn't want to die in a hospital or any kind of assisted living or hospice facility. So I began praying exactly that for him. I knew I had no control over how he would die and if he would need hospitalization or to be in hospice. So I prayed that he wouldn't need any of those things.

My dad eventually moved in with my sister and her family because they needed him to be there when their children got home from school. They lived just a few miles from us, so we still saw him often. I continued praying for him according to what he asked.

On the day he died, he got up and prepared his breakfast while everyone else in the house was sleeping, as he often did. Only this time he went back to bed—which was unusual for him—and never woke up. He died peacefully in his sleep, just the way he wanted to. He was 93 years old. He was not sick. Just frail and tired.

I had already had the talk with him about receiving Jesus, and he assured me that not only had he believed in and received Jesus, but he thought anyone who hadn't was stupid. I assured him that I did not suspect he was stupid, but I just wanted to make sure he was in heaven when I got there. He appreciated that. His mind was sharp and clear, and on the day he died I know he must have been wondering why he felt badly enough to go back to bed after breakfast.

Several close friends and family members have battled cancer valiantly but lost the fight. One of them in particular relieved any fear I had about the dying process. In fact, God used her experience to set me free of the fear of death. She and I had been faithful friends and prayer partners for decades, and we prayed about everything. We were very close and knew each other well. She was not my friend from high school, for that friend died early in her life as a believer.

Once my decades-long prayer partner was diagnosed with cancer, my husband and I prayed almost daily for her recovery. I prayed with her many times as well. But at the end she went downhill rapidly and succumbed to the disease far faster than any of us was prepared for.

I was not there on the day she died at home, but her immediate family was. I heard afterward from one of the family members I knew well that she had quickly become weaker and weaker and fell into a coma with no response. When that happened, the nurse who was staying with her and the family said they should call an ambulance to take her to hospice right away. She had not made a sound or opened her eyes or breathed normally for a number of hours.

As they were making that call in another room, one of her female family members went to check on her. When she entered my friend's room, my friend was sitting up in her bed, her eyes were wide open and looking as if she was seeing something magnificent. Her mouth was open with a broad smile, and she was breathing normally. Her family member ran to get the others to come and see her miraculous recovery, but when they arrived back in her room just a few moments later, she had passed away. But she still had a peaceful smile on her face.

Because I knew her and her family members so well, just hearing that story transformed my attitude about death. In the last moments before she died, she obviously saw an awesome scene. Was it angels? Was it other family members who had gone before her to be with the Lord? Was it the Lord Himself? Or all of the above? I don't know, but I know it was glorious. And she was happy about it.

Something happened to me the moment I heard that, and it has not changed one bit in those years since then. I know she saw something that no one else could see, and it was real. I expect to see the same thing or something similar when I go to be with the Lord. I expect to see Jesus. Or God's magnificent angels. Or loved ones. I pray for all my family members to see that same wonderful sight when they go to be with Him. Paul, who saw Jesus Himself, said of believers that if we are absent from the body we are present with the Lord (2 Corinthians 5:8). That sounds instantaneous to me. It doesn't sound as if we're trapped in some holding station while our future hangs in the balance.

I continue to pray that when it is my time to go be with the Lord that it is a peaceful passing, full of God's presence and the presence of His Spirit so strong that those with me will sense that too, even if they cannot see it. I believe that death is nothing to be feared, only to be welcomed and celebrated when the time comes. It's spectacular. Glorious. And, shall I say...heavenly.

Stephen was being martyred for his faith in Jesus, and the Roman people were stoning him to death. God allowed Stephen to see where he was going. "He, being full of the Holy Spirit, *gazed into heaven and saw the glory of God,* and Jesus standing at the right hand of God, and said, 'Look! *I see the heavens opened and the Son of Man standing at the right hand of God!*'" (Acts 7:55-56). That is powerful! What was set before him was far greater than what he was leaving behind.

Because we have invited the Lord to live in us, we walk in the Spirit. Because we have asked God to fill us and our days with Himself, we have His love, peace, and joy in our heart. Because we *praise Him* for all He has done for us, and *worship Him* for who He is, and *thank Him* for sharing Himself with us, now we can walk so closely with Him that we know He will keep His promise to never leave us nor forsake us. Never!

If we include God in everything we do and everything that happens to us, we will truly walk with Him in peace, and our relationship with Him will be so close that we are certain He will be with us in our departure from earth.

David prayed, "Yea, *though I walk through the valley of the shadow of death, I will fear no evil; for You are with me*; Your rod and Your staff, they comfort me" (Psalm 23:4). He knew God was with him. We have to know that too. Ask God to deliver you from the fear of death.

In order to overcome the fear of death, you must know who and what you believe without any doubting. That is good reason for you to keep learning about God, what Jesus did for you, and how the Holy Spirit moves in your life. Paul said, "I am not ashamed, for *I know whom I have believed* and am persuaded that *He is able to keep what I have committed to Him* until that Day" (2 Timothy 1:12).

Remember, the more you worship God on earth, the more you will feel right at home with the hosts of heaven worshipping Him around His throne. It will be a great homecoming, and you will fit right in.

If you are fearful of, or dreading, a loved one's death, especially if you are not certain of their eternal future because you don't know whether they know the Lord, remember this: "*Whoever calls on the name of the Lord shall be saved*" (Romans 10:13). If you have already lost a loved one, and to your knowledge that person did not know Jesus, you don't know for certain whether he or she called upon the name of the Lord. It may be just before they died—as they were about to be killed in an accident or destroyed by a disease. We don't know how many people have asked Jesus to save them on their deathbed. Even some of those in a coma can still hear people talking at their bedside. They no longer have control over their body, but they can still think. We do not know if they are thinking, *Jesus save me. Forgive me. Take me home with You.* Jesus already made the way for their salvation. They only have to open their heart to receive Him.

"Whoever calls on the name of the Lord shall be saved" is simple and clear. This is a great comfort to those of us who have lost loved ones without knowing if they were saved. You don't know for certain that you won't see your loved one or family member in heaven. You will have to wait until you get there to find out. Only God and they know for certain. But you can have hope and peace in the process. That's why I say, let's keep praying for those we see to receive Jesus. I have a couple of extended family members I pray for all the time. My prayer is, "Don't let them die without knowing You, Lord." I believe He will answer that prayer.

Don't Be Afraid of the End Times

The details of the end times in Revelation are scary. What frightens people most is how they could possibly live through it and how they might die. No one wants to go through what is described in the Bible. Many of us believers in Christ see the end times coming closer with each passing day. We observe how nations are positioning themselves against one another. We see the possibility of financial collapse because ungodly leaders have made horrible and unwise decisions that have led to our current situation. We see how in the chaos and financial upset the antichrist will rise up into power—because people with worldly wisdom will put him there. People with godly wisdom will see what is coming.

In order to know more of what is coming, you need to read Revelation, the last book in the Bible. It tells of the horrible things that will happen. But it also tells of the great things ahead for God's children.

Jesus said to His faithful people, "*Because you have kept My command to persevere, I also will keep you from the hour of trial which shall come upon the whole world*, to test those who dwell on the earth. Behold, I am coming quickly! Hold fast what you have, that no one may take your crown" (Revelation 3:10-11). Jesus will keep those who love Him and keep His commandments from experiencing the worst of what is to come. I believe Him.

Jesus also said, "*Behold, I stand at the door and knock. If anyone hears My voice and opens the door, I will come in to him and dine with him, and he with Me. To him who overcomes I will grant to sit with Me on My throne*, as I also overcame and sat down with My Father on His throne" (Revelation 3:20-21).

The tribulation period is the upsetting and trouble-filled times leading up to the rapture and the return of Christ. It is said in the Bible of those who come out of the tribulation, "*These are the ones who come out of the great tribulation, and washed their robes and made them white in the blood of the Lamb.* Therefore *they are before the throne of God*, and serve Him day and night in His temple. And He who sits on the throne will dwell among them. *They shall neither hunger anymore nor thirst anymore*; the sun shall not strike them, nor any heat; *for the Lamb who is in the midst of the throne will shepherd them and lead them to living fountains of waters.* And *God will wipe away every tear* from their eyes" (Revelation 7:14-17). What a wonderful promise to us all.

Many people will be deceived because they don't fear God. We can see this happening now. We see people in whom is the spirit of the antichrist.

"Then I heard a loud voice saying in heaven, "Now *salvation*, and *strength*, and *the kingdom of our God*, and *the power of His Christ* have come, for the accuser of our brethren, who accused them before our God day and night, has been cast down. And they overcame him by the blood of the Lamb and by the word of their testimony, and *they did not love their lives to the death*" (Revelation 12:10-11). The believers love Him so much they do not fear death.

Jesus said, "Behold, I am coming as a thief. Blessed is he who watches, and keeps his garments, lest he walk naked and they see his shame" (Revelation 16:15). We must stay strong with the Lord and be watchful in prayer and in His Word so we don't get off the path God has for us, and we are where we are supposed to be, doing what we are supposed to be doing, at all times.

There will be a great earthquake worse than any ever seen on the earth. (See Revelation 16:18.) But I do not believe that we who are believers in Christ now will be there to experience that. I cannot begin to explain in this short space what I believe about that and why I believe it. But read Revelation for yourself—not just once but many times—and decide what you believe. I believe that we who love, follow, and serve the Lord will not suffer the worst of what is to come. That's because of His great love for us and mercy toward us. We will go to be with Him before the final judgments. In the meantime, He will protect and provide for us. All I know is when it's my time to be with Him in heaven, I will be. And so will you. And He will be with us all the way.

Do not fear what is to come. The book of Revelation is not about when these things are going to happen; it's about what you and I are going to do to prepare for heaven. We don't need to nail down a date. We need to walk with faith in God; in purity of body, soul, and mind; and in love for God, our Lord and Savior, Jesus, and God's precious Holy Spirit. *Refuse to be afraid. God is with you forever. You can trust Him on that.*

Keep in mind that this world is temporary and will not always be here. Our lives in this world are stressful, and there are many distractions. We must do our best to focus on the Lord and our walk with Him. Jesus said, "He who hears My word and believes in Him who sent Me has everlasting life, *and shall not come into judgment, but has passed from death into life*" (John 5:24).

The best news is if the Spirit of Him who raised Jesus from the dead dwells in you, then it is guaranteed that He will raise you as well. (See Romans 8:11.)

God raises us up to live with Him forever when we die. What a great and precious hope this is for us. Do not fear the end times. Trust Him who is able to raise you from the dead to live in heaven with Him forever.

Prayer Power

Lord, I pray You will prepare me to be with You some-day in heaven. Take away any fear I have about that. I pray I will not die in some horrible, tragic, awful, suffering death. I pray I can die peacefully, surrounded by loving family members and friends. Usher me into Your presence in a way that allows others to see Your glory and goodness. I know that "to be absent from the body" is to be present with You (2 Corinthians 5:8). I look forward to being in Your presence forever.

Thank You that because I have received You as my Lord, my name is written in the Lamb's Book of Life. I pray it will be true of my family members as well. I pray that none of them will die without knowing You. In the meantime, help me to live the life You have for me in such a way that I am well prepared to be with You in heaven. I want to hear You say, "Well done my good and faithful servant." Only You can enable me to do that.

During the moments before my death, I pray I will see a glorious vision of You, Jesus, or the angels You have sent to usher me into Your presence. Use me to show others who are with me that there is nothing to fear in death—and that death is a new and glorious beginning with You and the believers and saints who have gone before us to be with You.

In Jesus' name I pray.

WORD POWER

God will redeem my soul from the power of the grave,
for He shall receive me.

PSALM 49:15

We are always confident,
knowing that while we are at home in the body
we are absent from the Lord. For we walk by faith, not by sight.
We are confident, yes, well pleased rather
to be absent from the body
and to be present with the Lord.

2 CORINTHIANS 5:6-8

If we live, we live to the Lord;
and if we die, we die to the Lord.
Therefore, whether we live or die, we are the Lord's.

ROMANS 14:8

If the Spirit of Him who raised Jesus
from the dead dwells in you,
He who raised Christ from the dead
will also give life to your mortal bodies
through His Spirit who dwells in you.

ROMANS 8:11

Let us hold fast the confession of
our hope without wavering,
for He who promised is faithful.

HEBREWS 10:23

10

What Can Keep Us from Fearing the Future?

Along with hearing from countless people all over the world who have been openly talking about the fear that is rampant in their own country, many people I see at various places I go now say such things as, "I am afraid of what is happening in the world." "I am afraid of the evil I see." "I'm afraid of the anger and hatred I see being acted out by far too many people." "I'm afraid that my son and daughter will not be safe at school." "I am afraid of having an accident or getting a terrible disease." "I'm afraid of dying of a heart attack and not being here to take care of my family." "I am afraid to be in a public place." "I am afraid of losing everything I have." "I'm afraid of what the doctor's report will be." "I am afraid of failing at what I do." "I am afraid that something bad will happen to me or my family." More and more I hear people say, "I'm afraid of everything." (Remember panophobia from the first chapter?)

The one fear I hear about most now is, "I am afraid of the future." "I'm afraid of what the future will bring." "I'm afraid of what the future will be for my children." "I don't want to have any children because I am afraid of all they will face in the future." That really says it all. If *we* are this afraid for *our* future and what it will be like for us and for our children, grandchildren, family, and friends, can we have a future worth living?

In order to have a good and successful future, we have to let go of the past and walk closely with God today. We have to make every fear we have about the future be a call to pray specifically regarding that. For example, if you are afraid for the safety of your children at their school, pray powerfully and fervently for that school. Find another parent or two, or five, or ten, and get together once a week or twice a month to pray about this. Pray for their teachers and the people who work at the school. Pray that no evil will enter the school, and if it's already there, pray that God will expose it and root it out. Pray that no weapon formed against any child, teacher, or staff member there will ever prosper. Put up a protective wall of prayer around all the children and the entire school. Tell God you want to exchange *your fear* for *His peace.* He will do that for you.

We must rise above any crippling fear we have of the future because it will cause us to run from all God has for us. Plus, it will please the enemy of our soul, who is always trying to rob us of our future. He wants to control our future so we will do his bidding. God says He has given us a good future. The following subsections concern things we can do to thwart any effort to take away our peace about the future.

Reject a Spirit of Self-Pity

We can't move successfully into the future God has for us as long as we are stuck in the past by self-pity. Self-pity is feeling sorry for ourselves. Feeling sorry for ourselves is sin. That's because it means we don't think God can change our situation or take care of our problems. We don't think God is enough. Self-pity is both doubt and worry. Doubt says, "I don't believe what God has said." Worry says, "I don't know if God can really help me." Doubt is the opposite of faith. Anything that is not from faith is sin. That's what the Bible says.

Self-pity is hard to recognize because it can manifest early in our lives when we experience negative conditions such as rejection, sadness, trauma, betrayal, or abuse. If we do not have the Lord closely in our lives, helping us to cope or recover—or we don't have a godly counselor talking us through it—we can easily end up entertaining a spirit of self-pity without even realizing it. Self-pity says, "I will always be hurt by others. I will always be mistreated. I will always fail. I will always lose."

I am certainly not sitting in judgment on anyone for having a spirit of self-pity, because I experienced it myself. But I am mentioning it here because it's a ploy of the enemy to keep us down and unable to rise above ourself and our situation. We can't soar into the future and purpose God has for us with this heavy weight on our shoulders. And I remember clearly the day I recognized it in myself.

Not long after Michael and I were married and I had received freedom from paralyzing depression and anxiety in the Christian counselor's office, a friend from church, who was a member of one of my prayer groups, told me that years ago she had been set free from a spirit of self-pity. I recognized that the reason she could have succumbed to those feelings was because of a group of tragedies she'd experienced. And I certainly understood why she would want to get free of that. But I never related any of what she was saying to my own life. Not at all. I never sat around feeling sorry for myself. I concentrated all my efforts into getting as far away from the past as I possibly could. But as she explained how getting rid of self-pity had changed her life dramatically for the better, I was intrigued. I thought how courageous she was to even admit that.

One day I was slighted publicly by a person giving credit to someone else for work I had done. Immediately, all the old, familiar, negative thoughts started playing in my head. "You are not important enough or worthy enough to ever be treated fairly by anyone." "You will never be appreciated." "You are not enough and never will be." I quickly descended into sadness and depression and felt like crying, but I had to hold back tears because…well, I was in public.

I prayed silently, *Lord, how long will I let the things people say and do affect me like this?* And God showed me instantly, in a flash of revelation to my mind, that I was entertaining a spirit of self-pity. I was believing lies promoted by the enemy of my soul that said, "Poor me. I am lacking, and nothing will ever change that." "Poor me. No one loves me enough to stand up for me." "Poor me. I will always be beaten down." "Poor me. I am always rejected because I am rejectable." "Poor me. I am not loved because I am unlovable." "Poor me. I will always be sad and never happy." "Poor me. I am destined to continually attract abusive people." "Poor me. I will never be able to get ahead." "Poor me. I never receive answers to my prayers." "Poor me. I always have things going wrong in my life." "Poor me. God loves everyone else more than me." "Poor me. I am destined to always fail." "Poor me. I always lose at everything." "Poor me! Poor me! Poor me!"

I realized I was accepting those negative thoughts as if they were God's revelation for my life. It was how I always felt at any sign of rejection or mistreatment by anyone. It was an old familiar feeling that descended on me like an oppressive blanket of sadness and grief. It wasn't God. It was a familiar spirit from the enemy that controlled me. It was fear that I would never be loved and accepted. And it had been with me so long that I thought, *This is just the way I am.*

The day I realized all this was the day I said, "No more! No more will I listen to that familiar spirit trying to talk me into thinking, *Poor me! No one will ever love, appreciate, understand, or see me. I will always be rejected, abused, unappreciated, mistreated, and unloved.* No more will I sink into a depressed sadness. I am done with all that. I resist those lies of the enemy, and I will only trust the truth of what God and His Word say about me."

From then on I was able to recognize that familiar spirit right away, and I could resist it by proclaiming the truth of God's Word. I refused to allow those lies to keep me in victim mode. Each time that happened, I said, "I am free in Christ, and He has healed me from negative thoughts. I will not replay those old tapes from the past that operate like an ever-revolving loop in my mind."

I praised God for that clear insight, saying, "Praise You, Lord, that You are the *way*, the *truth*, and the *life*. Thank You that *You* have restored my soul and made me whole. I will not fear what man can do to me. I will worship and reverence only *You*, for *You* are my life. *Your* ways are the way I want to live. I refuse to listen to deception and lies of the enemy. I choose to receive only *Your* truth. *You* have accepted me. *You* died for me. *You* have redeemed my life from the pit of hell I was living in. *You* have restored me. *You* will continue to deliver me. I reject those old feelings of rejection and self-pity. I confess them as sin against You. I see them as doubt that You love me or care about me, as if You aren't enough for me. Forgive me for believing lies instead of believing what *You* say about me. Thank You for showing me the truth." I did that every time I felt those old feelings descend on me, and eventually the spirit of self-pity left completely.

Feeling sorry for ourselves is a sin because it is a sign we doubt the goodness of God toward us.

The list of "Poor Me's" is endless. Self-pity is an easy attitude to slip into without even realizing it's opposed to everything God has for us.

In fact, it's in opposition to God's plan for our life. God wants us to forget about the past and move with Him into the future He has for us. We can't do that as long as we drag our list of "Poor Me's" along with us.

The enemy has no power in our lives unless we give it to him.

Ask God to show you if you ever fall into the bad habit of self-pity. If so, instead of believing lies from the enemy, declare the truth of God. Don't say, "Poor me. I should have more, I should be treated better, and I should not have to go through this." Say instead, "Thank You, God, that You love me, and You have accepted me, and You provide everything I need and always will."

Don't say, "Poor me. Nothing I do ever works out. I always fail." Instead say, "I can do all things through Christ who strengthens me. I am ultimately destined for success because God's Spirit is in me and leading me, and He never fails."

Don't allow yourself to be the devil's victim. I am not saying that nothing bad or difficult won't ever happen to you, but don't live in victimhood as if God isn't greater than what you experience. Victimhood may have been your past, or it may be your condition at this moment, but do not allow it to be your future. Or your future will be filled with fear, along with anger, resentment, hatred, and envy. Who wants to live that way?

Perpetual victimhood is a plan of the enemy of your soul. God's will for you is liberation and restoration. Don't limit God by listening to old, tired tapes proclaiming the enemy's lies. And don't listen to other people who want to keep you down by playing the "Poor victim" tapes they have for you so you can never rise above your circumstances. God doesn't think, *Poor little victim!* when He looks at you. He thinks of how much He wants to bless you and how much more He has for you. Say, "No! I refuse the lies of the enemy. From now on I am believing what God says about me."

Decide What You Believe and Stick to It

Our future is determined by what we believe. God asks us to live by faith in Him and His Word. If something happens to threaten my safety or well-being, and I start to fret and worry instead of going to God and thanking Him that He is the Lord of my life and He is my protector and provider, it shows I do not live in faith. It reveals I have serious doubt that God is actually more powerful than anything I face.

Decide what you believe:

Either Jesus *is* who He said He is, or He is *not*.

Either Jesus *spoke* the truth, or He *did not*.

Either God's *Word* is true, or it is *not*.

If you answered "*He is*," "*He did*," and "*It is*," then don't let those beliefs waver. Say this out loud whenever doubt about these truths starts to creep into your thinking: "I have decided to follow Jesus. No turning back, no turning back."

What we decide doesn't determine if something is true or not. For example, if you decide that Jesus is not who He said He was, that doesn't make it true. Jesus is still who He said He is, but the reality of who He is will not be affecting your life in a glorious and transforming way because you have rejected Him.

If you do not trust the Word of God—which contains the truth and promises Jesus spoke, tells of the love God has for you, and teaches you the dependability of His ways—you will always be afraid that God won't come through for you. Even though time and again in the New and Old Testaments there are great examples of God keeping His promises to His people—whether *good* because of their faith, humility, and obedience, or *bad* because of their doubt, pride, and disobedience.

God doesn't want us to always be thinking about the worst-case scenario for our lives. He wants us to read His Word, pray to Him, and stand firm on His promises so we can anticipate the best that is yet to come.

God cares about every aspect of your life—physical, mental, emotional, and spiritual. He cares about our basic needs. Jesus said, "Do not worry about your life, what you will eat or what you will drink; nor about your body, what you will put on. Is not life more than food and the body more than clothing?" (Matthew 6:25). *God also cares about the quality and length of your life—your past, present, and future.* In all of our life, He says, "Do not be anxious." "Do not worry." "Do not be afraid."

We all want to have some control over what happens to us and our family. God knows that. That's why He has given us His Word, prayer, praise, and worship so we can have a close relationship with Him. When we invite God to be Lord of our lives and then submit everything to Him in prayer, *we* are in control of our decision to put *Him* in control. *We* decide. *We* choose. That is the only way to keep our life from getting *out* of control.

Worry means we have not truly given a person or situation to God. It doesn't mean you are not a believer. It doesn't mean you're not saved. It doesn't mean you are going to hell. It just means you need to get closer to God—in prayer, praise, worship, and in His Word. Ask God to give you His peace by the power of His Spirit within you. Refuse to live as though God doesn't exist in your life. Refuse to entertain negative thoughts as though Jesus didn't die for you and the Spirit of God doesn't live in you. Refuse to live as if you have no hope. God says He wants your hope to be in Him.

Determine Today What Your Future Will Be

The way we walk with God today will determine what our future will be. Walking our own way—*without* God—takes us off the path we need to be on. Walking *with* God and drawing closer to Him each day keeps us on the right path to where we need to go.

If you are walking with God, you must decide not to live in fear every day over whether you are good enough, acceptable enough, and smart enough or destined for failure, rejection, and humiliation. If you are doing that, your assignment is: Stop listening to those lies! Those very fears are planted and fed by the enemy of your soul, and they are intended to torture you and bring you down. They are in direct opposition to what God says about you. He says you are *good* and *acceptable* and *loved* because He sees the righteousness and beauty of Jesus when He looks at you. He sees His Holy Spirit in you, enabling you to be all He created you to be. He has given you the mind of Christ and gifted You with wisdom and knowledge because you have trusted in Him and have reverenced Him in your heart. And other people will see it as well, even if they don't know what it is.

Fearing the future is torture. You don't have to live that way. You don't have to dread the future or be afraid of bad news when it comes. You can run to God and hide yourself in Him. The Bible says of believers in the one true God, "Surely *he will never be shaken; the righteous will be in everlasting remembrance. He will not be afraid of evil tidings; his heart is steadfast, trusting in the Lord*" (Psalm 112:6-7).

When you are afraid of the future, say, "God is with me. He will never leave me or forsake me. His Spirit is in me giving me peace, guidance, and joy even in difficult times." Even when bad things are happening to you and around you that you don't understand, remember that God shares His presence with you as you surrender your life to Him in prayer, praise, worship, and faith in His Word.

Remember, your future is determined by the steps you take today.

Five Things to Remember When Thinking About Your Future

1. *Remember that God's Holy Spirit is always within you.* Having the Holy Spirit in you is how Jesus never leaves you nor forsakes you. So when times and situations become dark around you and you are afraid, remember that you always have the light of the world in you no matter what is happening. I am not saying you will never be afraid. I'm saying God doesn't want you to *live* that way. At the first sign of fear, *run to God*, knowing His Spirit in you gives you a direct line to your heavenly Father.

2. *Remember that God gave you a brain and told you how to use it.* Depending on God and listening to Him for guidance does not mean you never need your brain again. He gives you godly wisdom, understanding, revelation, and a sound mind. He also gives you a choice. Your mind receives what He gives you, and your will and brain make the decisions. He wants your brain and your will to be submitted to *Him*.

All this does not mean that you allow yourself or a family member to be abused. Remember what I said about good fear? If you or your family is in danger, ask God what you should do about it. Should you leave the situation, or the place, or the neighborhood, or the person or persons? If a family member is putting you in danger, do not allow that person to do anything to harm you or your children. Find help. Get out of any danger. Your future depends on it.

We often wait for God to acknowledge our frightening situation, while He waits for us to acknowledge Him and invite Him to work powerfully in our situation.

3. *Remember that God wants you to ask Him about the future.* God has ultimately prepared a future better for you than anything you have

ever seen, or heard, or thought of, or even hoped for yourself. And He doesn't necessarily give you specific details or timetables about your future, but He will give you what you need to know when you need to know it. But seek Him for it. He said, "Ask Me of things to come" (Isaiah 45:11). He wants to share certain knowledge with you about the future, but you have to seek Him for it. He will *always* give you the assurance that your future is in His hands, and you are to pray and ask Him to guide you into it.

It's always wise to think about the future and evaluate where we are headed. The Bible says Jerusalem was destroyed because *"she did not consider her future. Her fall was astounding, there was none to comfort her"* (Lamentations 1:9 NIV). That doesn't mean the people forgot to think about the future. It means they did bad things without a thought to what God had told them regarding the consequences they would face if they were unrepentant and *kept on* living that way.

Too many people live each day without much thought as to what will happen in their future if they keep on doing what they are doing. They don't consider the consequences of the way they are living. The people in Jerusalem who didn't consider their future didn't consider their God either. They were not walking with God and therefore were mindless of the consequences that were coming upon them. The consequences, I must add, that God had made clear to them many times. Tell God what you fear about the future and ask Him to guide you and walk you through it step-by-step each day. Tell Him that *He* is your future, and you believe everything He says in His Word about you and the future He has for you.

4. *Remember that when you make plans for your future, do not leave God out of them.* God should be consulted on all your plans so that *your* future plans are perfectly aligned with *His*. We aren't supposed

to conjure up a vision for our lives and *then ask God to bless it.* We are supposed to *first ask God what His plans are for our lives*, and then ask Him to *lead* us as we walk into our future with Him every day.

We all make plans for our next meal, where we will live, what we need to do to live safely and take care of our children and family. God wants us to make plans, but He doesn't want us to do that without consulting Him first. "A man's heart plans his way, but the LORD directs his steps" (Proverbs 16:9). God doesn't want us to assume too much before checking with Him. Besides, if we look too far ahead in the future, we can become afraid of all the possibilities that *could* happen, or *might not* happen, and that adds to our fear.

Bring every fear or concern to God and pray until you receive peace about it. If you don't have peace, keep on praying. Once you do have peace, leave it in His hands so you can rest at night.

5. *Remember that God is never overwhelmed.* Although we may feel overwhelmed about the future, God is not. We may feel panic about what tomorrow brings, but He is not panicked. He is in control. Any fear you have should lead you to pray and give it to God. He will enable you to let it go and trust Him more. That is how you put Him back in control of your life and allow Him to take away your fear. Feeling overwhelmed means there is something you are not trusting God for in your life.

What Is a Good Future, Anyway?

Too many people have their own idea of what a good future is. Some think being rich, famous, successful, and admired is a good future, but few people can handle that without becoming prideful and independent of God. They buy into what the world has to offer, and it comes up short. That's why God often waits for us to get clarity regarding what a good future really means.

A good future is living in God's presence according to His will and safe from the plans of evil. It's being able to provide for our family and for other people as God puts them on our heart and in our life. It includes having good, godly relationships and strong family ties. It's having priorities that put God first above all else. It's giving to God what He requires and being blessed because you have done so. It's living in a safe and peaceful place, and having good work to do, while being enabled by God to do it well.

A good future is something you walk into every day as you walk with God.

Noah, Abraham, and Moses did amazing and great things because they walked with God closely enough to hear His call on their lives and to understand each day what steps they were to take.

God blessed *Noah* because "Noah walked with God" and did what God instructed him to do every day (Genesis 6:9). Imagine if Noah heard the astounding things God was calling him to do and then said, "Okay God, I've got this. I'll take it from here."

What if Noah would have tried to build that enormous ark without God's plans and help? It had to be built perfectly in order to survive the enormous deluge that was coming in the future. And Noah needed to find two of every kind of animal—male and female—and get them on the boat with the food and supplies they would need to survive all those days. What if he only found one of some species? But God *sent* the animals to him.

God told *Abraham*, "Get out of your country, from your family and from your father's house, to a land that I will show you. I will make you a great nation; I will bless you and make your name great; and you shall be a blessing. I will bless those who bless you, and I will curse him who curses you; and in you all the families of the earth shall be blessed" (Genesis 12:1-3).

What if Abraham had said, "Okay, Lord, I can do this. I'll call You if I need You." Abraham would never have left town because he didn't even know where he was going. How would he know when he had arrived without the Lord showing him? How would he have made himself a great and blessed nation? No one does that without God.

God spoke to *Moses* and said, "I have surely seen the oppression of My people who are in Egypt, and have heard their cry because of their taskmasters, for I know their sorrows. So I have come down to deliver them out of the hand of the Egyptians, and to bring them up from that land to a good and large land, to a land flowing with milk and honey" (Exodus 3:7-8). Then God told Moses that He wanted *him* to do it.

What if Moses had said, "No problem. I'll take care of it. See You in the Promised Land." No one would have made it out of Egypt, especially since he was already wanted for murdering an Egyptian. So the first time Moses tried to get in to see Pharaoh without any special signs and wonders from God indicating that God was with him, Moses wouldn't have made it out alive.

What if Noah, Abraham, and Moses had looked far into the future and said to God, "I can't see how this can ever happen. I don't want to even try. I'm exhausted just hearing about it." Nothing would have ever been done.

We can't look too far into the future either. We need to walk closely with God the way these great men did. They knew they were being asked to do monumental things they couldn't possibly do on their own. They knew they needed the guidance, knowledge, and enablement from the Lord to do it. We need to know that too.

When you walk with the Lord, He will lead you into all He has for you. It won't always look like what you had in mind, but be open to what He is leading you to do. When you live with a sense of

God's purpose, you won't just wander around, hoping for the best and fearing the worst. You will have a clear sense that you are either in the right place at the right time or you are not. And you need to have that clarity and assurance, because God may be allowing you to experience fear for the purpose of drawing you closer to Him so you can hear what He is instructing you to do next. Your close walk with God and your sense of purpose will clearly indicate to you the boundaries of your life. And that makes your choices so much easier.

There will always be something to be afraid of in your life. The call of God can be scary too. Just ask Jesus. Keep walking closely with God and surrender any fear you have about the future by taking each one to God in prayer. Then keep waiting on Him as your heart, mind, and soul become settled in peace. He wants you to trust that He has a future for you and that it is good.

Don't Listen to Godless People Telling You What Your Future Will Be

As I started having fearful thoughts while writing this book, I asked God to show me any place in my life where I was living below the level He had for me. I quickly saw that I was listening to frightening news reports more than I was listening to Him. I was paying attention to terrible predictions more than I was to the precious promises of God.

The Bible says we must not walk in the counsel of ungodly people. That's because they don't know the real truth. They cannot predict the future. Only God *knows* the future. And because they are godless, they don't know the power of prayer in Jesus' name. Prayer changes things, and polls don't factor into that consideration. The thing we know for sure is that the more people reject God, the more godless they become in rebelling against Him. And this grows as we get closer to the return of Christ.

We cannot swim in the depressing predictions of a world that doesn't acknowledge God. They will drown us in fear. They don't know the extraordinary world of God's kingdom, where all things are possible. So put all your expectations in the Lord and not in other people. "My soul, wait silently for God alone, for my expectation is from Him" (Psalm 62:5).

God never lets us stay where we are in our relationship with Him. There is always room for us to become more like Him. The truth is, if we are not moving forward with the Lord, we are sliding backward. And God doesn't allow backsliding. That undermines His plans for our lives.

God will always have a new time and a new beginning ahead for you. This will bring you to a new degree of commitment to Him; a new sense of your purpose and calling; a new level of prayer and intercession; and a fresh dedication to serving God, your family, your spouse, your children, and the people He has put in your life. This is all part of becoming everything He created you to be and living the life He has for you. So shut off the TV and pick up the Bible if you are feeling fearful about the future. The world doesn't have the answers. God does.

Know That Your Future Is with the Lord

When Jesus was telling His disciples about His coming death, He said, "*He who believes in Me, the works that I do he will do also; and greater works than these he will do, because I go to My Father. And whatever you ask in My name, that I will do, that the Father may be glorified in the Son. If you ask anything in My name, I will do it*" (John 14:12-14). Because we have received Jesus, we can accomplish great and amazing things when we pray in His name.

Because of Jesus we have a direct connection to God. By receiving Him, we are receiving an *unshakeable kingdom*. Jesus said, "*The kingdom of heaven is like treasure hidden in a field*, which a man found and hid; and for joy over it he goes and sells all that he has and buys that field. Again, *the kingdom of heaven is like a merchant seeking beautiful pearls*, who, when he had found one pearl of great price, went and sold all that he had and bought it" (Matthew 13:44-46).

This means we must see the kingdom of heaven as more valuable than anything else. And we should pay whatever price it takes to obtain it.

Paul talked about his future, saying, "A great and effective door has opened to me, and *there are many adversaries*" (1 Corinthians 16:9). When you move into the greater work the Lord has for you, expect adversaries, because the enemy will show up to oppose you with fear, uncertainty, and doubt.

Remember that "He who is in you is greater than he who is in the world" (1 John 4:4) so resist the enemy, and he will flee from you.

Paul asked, "Who shall separate us from the love of Christ? Shall tribulation, or distress, or persecution, or famine, or nakedness, or peril, or sword?" (Romans 8:35). He answered his question, saying, "I am persuaded that *neither death nor life*, nor angels nor principalities nor powers, nor things present nor things to come, nor height nor depth, nor any other created thing, *shall be able to separate us from the love of God* which is in Christ Jesus our Lord" (Romans 8:38-39). That means nothing can separate you from God's love. Not now. Not ever.

The more evil proliferates, the more we want the return of Jesus to come soon. But Jesus didn't tell His disciples to stand there waiting for Him to return. He told them, "It is not for you to know times or seasons which the Father has put in His own authority" (Acts 1:7). We don't have to know everything that will happen in the future. We just have to know the Lord. *He* is our future. We don't have to know what will happen or *when* it will happen. We just need to know that we will be with Him always, no matter what happens.

"If God is for us, who can be against us?" (Romans 8:31). God *is* for you. He was for you before you were even born. And because of that, He will complete the process in you until you are glorified in His presence with your spiritual body in eternity.

Run the Race with God, Knowing He Has Set You Up to Win It

In the meantime, before Jesus returns, He wants us to live our lives in a way that is pleasing to Him and fulfilling His purpose for us. He wants us to run the race to win it. "Do you not know that those who run in a race all run, but one receives the prize? Run in such a way that you may obtain it. And everyone who competes for the prize is temperate in all things. Now they do it to obtain a perishable crown, but *we for an imperishable crown*" (1 Corinthians 9:24-25).

When we finally see the Lord in eternity, we want to hear, "*Well done, good and faithful servant; you were faithful over a few things, I will make you ruler over many things. Enter into the joy of your lord*" (Matthew 25:21). That's why we discipline ourselves to always do the right thing—to be like Christ as much as we are able, no matter what is going on. "*The steps of a good man are ordered by the* Lord, and He delights in his way*" (Psalm 37:23). The good news is that the Holy Spirit in us helps us to do the right thing.

God wants us to live in unity with our brothers and sisters in Christ. He wants us to live in peace with unbelievers too, as much as we are able. We should never commit the prideful sin of looking down on other races or cultures of people. We are all one blood. "*He has made from one blood every nation of men to dwell on all the face of the earth*" (Acts 17:26). God wants us to remember that there are only two types of people in the world—those who are saved and those who are not. For those who are not, we have good news, and God wants us to share it. Human fear is a dark place where our doubt covers over the full light of the Lord in us.

God is saying to you, "Arise, shine; for your light has come! And the glory of the LORD is risen upon you. For behold, the darkness shall cover the earth, and deep darkness the people; *but the LORD will arise over you, and His glory will be seen upon you*" (Isaiah 60:1-2).

When God put it on my heart to write this book on fear, the world was not as dangerous as it is today. The spread of evil was not as immense and far reaching. But God knew the world would be like it is now. In fact, He described it in His Word. But we cannot crawl in a cave and think we and our family will be safe. We can't live in a bubble apart from atrocities occurring all over the world. The world will reach us. That's why we have to keep praying that good, godly people come to power in every country, city, town, and community. We have to pray that godless and evil people will be taken out of power. We must pray every day that all of the evil the enemy is planning will not come to pass, and that God's plans to protect righteous believers in Him will prevail.

I say, "Let us lay aside every weight, and the sin which so easily ensnares us, and let us run with endurance the race that is set before us" (Hebrews 12:1).

We can do this because the Holy Spirit enables us to serve God and do His will. People need to know that they can spend eternity with the Lord. And He will be with them on earth until that time. No one knows for sure when He is coming back, yet we can certainly see the signs of that more clearly than ever before. But it is enough to know He is coming, and we will be with Him when we die or when He returns—whichever comes first.

When Jesus was walking on the water to meet the disciples on their boat, He knew they were afraid, so He reassured them saying, "Be of good cheer! It is I; do not be afraid" (Matthew 14:27). They didn't really know who was with them. You, too, need to recognize who is really with you. When the Lord says to you, "Do not be afraid, for I am with you," you can be completely certain He is.

Prayer Power

Lord, I thank You that You have given me "a future and a hope" (Jeremiah 29:11). Thank You that Your thoughts toward me are "of peace and not of evil." Thank You that because I love You and walk with You and live Your way, I have a good future ahead. Take away all my fears about the future. No matter what in the world I hear, help me to depend only on Your truth and Your love and power in my life. This is the day You have made; and I "will rejoice and be glad in it" (Psalm 118:24).

Thank You, Lord, that You are "a sun and shield" to me, and You "give grace and glory" and "no good thing" will You withhold "from those who walk uprightly" (Psalm 84:11). I want to be able to say, "I have fought the good fight, I have finished the race, I have kept the faith" (2 Timothy 4:7). I know that "in all these things" I am more than a conqueror through Jesus who loves me (Romans 8:37).

Thank You that "You will show me the path of life; in Your presence is fullness of joy; at Your right hand are pleasures forevermore" (Psalm 16:11). Thank You that because I have put my faith in You, I have Your Holy Spirit within me, and this seals my future. Help me to keep my eyes on You and not the predictors of disaster who don't know You. They don't determine my future—*You* do. Help me to forget "those things which are behind" and reach "forward to those things which are ahead" (Philippians 3:13).

In Jesus' name I pray.

WORD POWER

Mark the blameless man, and observe the upright;
for the future of that man is peace.

PSALM 37:37

I know the thoughts that I think toward you, says the LORD,
thoughts of peace and not of evil,
to give you a future and a hope.

JEREMIAH 29:11

I consider that the sufferings of this present time
are not worthy to be compared with the glory
which shall be revealed in us.

ROMANS 8:18

Everyone who asks receives, and he who seeks finds,
and to him who knocks it will be opened.

MATTHEW 7:8

Those who wait on the LORD shall renew their strength;
they shall mount up with wings like eagles,
they shall run and not be weary,
they shall walk and not faint.

ISAIAH 40:31

Other Books by Stormie Omartian

OUT OF DARKNESS

Stormie Omartian tells her compelling story of a childhood marred by physical and emotional abuse that eventually led her into the occult, drugs, and tragic relationships. Finding herself overwhelmed by fear and on the verge of suicide, she shares the turning point that changed her life and reveals the healing process that brought freedom and wholeness beyond what she ever imagined. In this poignant true story, there is help and hope for anyone who has been scarred by the past or feels imprisoned by deep emotional needs. It tells how God can bring life out of death, light out of darkness, hope out of hopelessness.

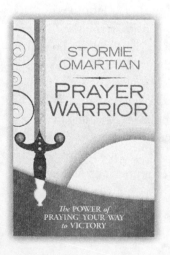

PRAYER WARRIOR

Stormie says, "There is already a war going on around you, and you are in it whether you want to be or not. There is a spiritual war of good and evil—between God and His enemy—and God wants us to stand strong on His side, the side that wins. We win the war when we pray in power because prayer *is* the way we do battle." This book will help you become a powerful prayer warrior who understands the path to victory.

LEAD ME, HOLY SPIRIT

Stormie provides a brand-new look at one of God's most amazing gifts to those who believe in Him: the Holy Spirit. You can walk in the power and presence of the Holy Spirit in every area of your life. With a sure hand, Stormie helps you to see that the Holy Spirit wants those who know Him to hear His gentle leading when He speaks to their heart, soul, and spirit. He wants to help believers enter into the relationship with God they yearn for, the wholeness and freedom God has for them, and the fulfillment of God's promises to them. He *wants* to lead them.

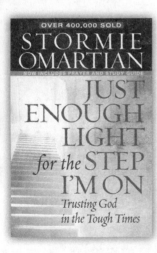

JUST ENOUGH LIGHT FOR THE STEP I'M ON

Anyone going through changes or difficult times will appreciate Stormie's honesty, candor, and advice based on the Word of God and her experiences in this book that is perfect for the pressures of today's world. She covers such topics as "Surviving Disappointment," "Walking in the Midst of the Overwhelming," "Reaching for God's Hand in Time of Loss," and "Maintaining a Passion for the Present," so you can "Move into the Future God Has for You."

To learn more about Harvest House books and
to read sample chapters, visit our website:

www.harvesthousepublishers.com

HARVEST HOUSE PUBLISHERS
EUGENE, OREGON